Text by **Chantal Bernard**

Foreword by **Anne Hudson**

DESSERTS

Basic techniques and the best recipes

Photography by **Sophie Boussahba**

Styling by **Emmanuelle Javelle**

First published 2005 under the title:
"Desserts. Le B.A.Ba de la pâtisserie"
by Kubik éditions
© Archipel studio and CEDUS, 2005

This edition © Kubik/RvR 2005
RvR Verlagsgesellschaft
Schulstr. 64
D-77694 Kehl
info@kubikinternational.de
www.kubikinternational.de

PUBLISHER: Jean-Jacques Brisebarre
DESIGN: Thomas Brisebarre

ENGLISH EDITION:
Produced by Silva Editions Ltd
PROJECT MANAGER: Sylvia Goulding
Translated by Jennifer Patterson
Text adapted for the English edition
by Lorna Brash

ISBN: 3-938265-16-7

Printed in Spain in April 2005

[Contents]

Foreword 5

THE SECRETS OF SUCCESS 6
Essential ingredients 8
Equipment 13
Tips and Tricks 14

SHORTCRUST PASTRY 20
Tarte Tatin 22
Sugar tart 22
Apricot custard tart 24
Rhubarb tart with speculoos 24
Custard flan 25

SABLÉE PASTRY 26
Fromage blanc gateau 28
Italian almond gateau 28
Raspberry tart gratinée 30
Chocolate fondant tart 30

PUFF PASTRY 32
Apricot tricornes 34
Apple and hazelnut turnovers 34
Puffed almond galette 36
Spiced apple tart 37
Savoyard pear rézules 37
Mille-feuilles 38

DOUGHNUT AND BEIGNET BATTER 40
Melon beignets 42
Chiquenaudes 42
Apple fritters 44
Madrid churros 45
Berlin doughnuts 45

CHOUX PASTRY 46
Chocolate éclairs 48
Paris-Brest 48
Gateau St Honoré 51
Cherry profiteroles 52
Easter egg croquembouche 52

CRÊPE, PANCAKE AND WAFFLE BATTER 54
Flambé crêpes with citrus butter 56
Vanilla crêpes 56
Pear soufflé crêpes 59
Lemon crêpe gateau 59
Orange-flower waffles 60
Dry waffles with brown sugar 60

MIXTURES THAT RISE AND THEIR VARIATIONS 62
Fruit cake 64
Rum baba 64
Gugelhupf 67
Lemon soufflé 67
Orange fondant cake 68
Doughnuts 68
Pound cake 69
Gateau de ménage 70
Carrot cake 70
Pamplona gateau 72
Yogurt and raisin gateau 72
Chocolate hazelnut brownies 73

BUTTERCREAM 74
Easter torte 76
Chestnut log 77
Summer fruit gateau 78

CUSTARD 80
Figs with almond cream 82
Chocolate marquise 82
Floating islands 85
Bavarian cream 85

PATISSERIE CREAM 86
Strawberry meringue gateau 88
Neopolitan sponge 89
Fresh fig gateau 90
Andalusian gateau 92
Strawberry and pistachio tart 93

WHIPPED CREAM 94
Coffee meringue gateau 96
Redcurrant amandine gateau 96
Small coffee pots 98
Fromage blanc with raspberry coulis 98
Exotic puits d'amour 101
Chocolate terrine with orange slivers 101

ICE CREAM 102
Rhubarb ice cream 104
Baked Alaska 104
Iced nougat with chicory coulis 107
Orange tutti-frutti cups 107
Iced cherry soufflé 108
Quick fruity ice cream log 109
Individual orange sorbets 110

Hot greengages with ice cream 110
Candied fruit bombe 112
Cassata 112
Rose ice cream 113

FRUIT DESSERTS 114
Fruit sabayon 116
Chocolate fondue 116
Exotic spiced fruit salad 117
Whole oranges with port 118
Tiered apple dessert 118
Summer fruit brochettes 120
Bananas en papillottes 120
Rhubarb charlotte 121
Red fruit crumble 122
Wok-fried bananas with caramel sauce 122
Cherry cheesecake 124
Roasted peaches with spiced bread 124
Baked apples 125
Ricotta gateau 126
Panellets 126
Pears in red wine 126
Candied fruit diplomate 128
Lemon rulade 128
Apple gateau (Apfelkuchen) 129

CLASSIC DESSERTS 130
Old-fashioned crème brûlée 132
Semolina and apricot gateau 132
Chocolate mousse 133
Meringues 133
Caramelised rice gateau 134
Cherry and rhubarb clafoutis 134
Individual egg custards 135
Black-Forest gateau 136
Tiramisu 136
Easter gateau with fruit and nuts 138
Crème caramel in ramekins 138
Breton Far 139
Simnel cake 139
Calfoutis of Pears Belle-Hélène 140
Gateau-madeleine 140
Rice pudding with cherry compote 141

Glossary 142
Index 143
Credits 144

[Foreword]

Desserts remind each and everyone of us of the golden days of childhood, of birthday parties and festivities.

As a child, no punishment saddened me more than the dreaded words "if you don't finish what's on your plate, you won't get any dessert!" This threat must have sparked my curiosity as well as my interest in food because I learned to taste everything and to like everything, even if it was sometimes difficult to swallow veal liver or split peas.

The ultimate gift at the end of a meal, desserts are presents given to us by each season: Spring is the time for Easter eggs, strawberry tarts and rose-flavoured ice creams... Summer, when we pick sweet ripe fruit, is the season for charlottes, clafoutis made with black cherries with the stones still in, fruit salads and sorbets. When autumn and the first cold spells return, rice pudding coated with caramel, floating islands capped with crisp spun caramel or apple tarts bring us their sweet comfort. Winter festivities invite us to enjoy an Advent cake with dried fruit, a Yule log with chestnut purée, a puff pastry frangipane pie or vanilla pancakes... These are desserts to be made and savoured according to seasonal produce and circumstances but also according to your own likes and dislikes.

For me, the queen of desserts is mille-feuilles, the real thing, with its puff pastry, its rich patisserie cream and its icing sugar... Especially the icing sugar! As a little girl – I still do it occasionally when nobody's watching – I used to take this beautiful slice made of flaky layers of pastry delicately covered with icing sugar, save it and only eat it right at the end. And invariably I would be left with a lovely sweet moustache... It was so good! And the small cream puffs whose fine golden robes run in large droplets down their sides...

This book makes classic and modern dessert recipes accessible to everyone. It enables us, like true pastry chefs, to produce all of these sweet treasures.

Desserts are the reward for our liking for food and the recipes and photographs in this book are themselves a magnificent treat.

With grateful thanks!
ANNE HUDSON

[The secrets

Creating a dessert, whether it is prepared in advance or takes just a few moments on the day, is something that anyone can do, especially when you are equipped with good recipes that you can follow to the letter. But if you wish to personalise a dessert, tart or mousse, you'll need to be familiar with the ingredients that it is made from, because you'll need to know before you use them, whether to choose caster or granulated or icing sugar? Pasteurised or unpasteurised milk? Single or double cream or crème fraîche? Wheat flour or corn flour? Plain or strong?

In the same way, then, that you keep a little oil, a tin of tuna and some dried pasta for emergencies, you can also keep a few essential ingredients to hand that allow you to create a dessert when unexpected guests arrive or to modify a classic recipe.

The successful outcome of a dessert is partly due to the tools you use to measure and prepare the ingredients. While a minimum number of kitchen utensils are necessary, these don't have to be state-of-the-art: expensive implements, tools such as spatulas, sieves, graters and various types of tins are often found lying around just crying out to be used more often. Once all the ingredients and various tools have been assembled, it is useful to know a few hints and tips to give yourself every chance of earning your stripes as a dessert chef; expert tips that may save time, repair a mishap, keep a dessert for longer... The following pages will yield a few secrets that enable you to cross over the threshold into the kingdom of sweets and to finish your everyday meals just like your festive menus with delicious desserts...

Essential ingredients

Sugar

Sugar comes in different forms, each is designed more for one particular use than another. Take good care to choose the right kind of sugar depending on what you want to use it for. The result will be the better for it. Here are the most important types to choose from.

Caster sugar ▸ This type of sugar dissolves rapidly. The most commonly used sugar for confectioning and making desserts, especially gateaux, creams, fruit salads, meringues, it is also used for sprinkling over pancakes, doughnuts and beignets after cooking.
•Take care not to add it all at once to egg yolks – it would make everything stick and hard to dissolve: sprinkle the sugar onto egg yolks while mixing. The sugar will have dissolved when the mixture has doubled in volume and turned creamy white.
•Add this sugar to pancake and waffle batter to make the pancake or waffle turn a golden colour during cooking. It also turns them slightly crisp.
•Before you flambé (set alight) a dessert (baked Alaska, fruits…), shake castor sugar over them: this will add a caramel flavour to that of the alcohol.

Granulated sugar ▸ This type of sugar has larger granules than caster sugar. It is used for making jam and various sweets, and helps to ensure that the gateau doesn't stick to the tin **(see p. 14)** and for decorating gateaux…

Icing sugar ▸ This is caster sugar ground very finely to a powder. It dissolves extremely fast but is sensitive to humidity. Use both to make icing and to decorate gateaux, as well as for making sablées and sugared pastry. It is also used to sweeten whipped cream and to make uncooked desserts such as mousses and petit-fours.

Sugar lumps ▸ These are made by compressing caster sugar granules –

this moulded white sugar is extremely absorbent and practical. Indispensable for successful caramel-making, sugar lumps also make it easier to add citrus flavouring to desserts as they can be rubbed against the zest. Brown sugar lumps are ideal for hot drinks. Small sugar cubes are great for making a punch.

Preserving sugar ▸ Mixed with natural fruit pectin and citric acid, this is, as its name suggests, ideal for making jams, marmalades and jellies as it obliterates the need to add pectin. It is also useful for making ice creams as it stops them from forming large crystals.

Demerara sugar ▸ The flavour of this Mauritian brown cane sugar with a 2% molasses content is reminiscent of rum. It is usually used for making exotic gateaux and to flavour fruit juices, punches and creams…

Light and dark brown soft sugar ▸ Light: A fine-grained and moist sugar, used for baking. Slight toffee fudge flavour but light in colour. Dark: A very fudgy, moist, fine-grained sugar with a dark-brown colour. Good for sticky sweets and chutneys, Northern France recipes and sugar tart **(see p. 22)**.

Molasses sugar ▸ This soft, moist, fine-grained sugar is full of natural molasses. Its distinctive dark brown almost black colour, colour and rich flavour make it suitable for Christmas all dark fruit cakes. Also very good in savoury dishes, such as chutneys, pickles and marinades.

Milk and Cream

Milk ▸ Various types of milk can be used interchangeably when making desserts: unpasturised milk (always boil this type for at least 5 minutes before using), pasteurised, sterilised,

tinned, powdered milk and sweetened or unsweetened concentrated milk.
Cream ▸ Only buy the quantity you need for the recipe you are about to make.

Double cream ▸ 48% fat – used in many desserts and gateaux – it can be used unwhipped in sauces and fillings or whipped as a topping or gateau filling. Alternatively, use full-fat crème fraîche as a replacement.

Whipped cream ▸ 35% fat – this is used in puddings and desserts, light mousses and profiteroles. Fromage frais can be used in its place.

Single cream ▸ 18% fat – normally homogenised to prevent separation. Single creams are mainly used as a pouring cream to serve as an accompaniment.

Crème fraîche ▸ Made by adding a culture to double cream, which thickens and gives it a sharp taste. High in fat, at around 40%, the same as double cream, it can be substituted for the latter. It withstands high heat and is therefore suitable for cooking. A half-fat version is available which has a slightly more tangy taste – however, take care when heating this as it is more likely to 'split' than its full-fat version.

Fromage frais & Fromage blanc ▸ Fromage blanc is a grainier version of fromage frais. Fromage frais is a soft unripened cheese, form which the whey has only partially been drained off to give a consistency of thick yogurt with a milky flavour. Both types of fromage are interchangeable. The fat content can range between 0–8% although it is sometimes enriched with cream. Fromage blanc is slightly more sour tasting and has a grainier texture. Allow hot sauces to cool slightly before adding either of these cheese to prevent separation.

Cereals

Wheat flour ▶ Wholewheat, plain flour, self-raising flour, wholemeal and strong plain flour are just some of the derivatives of wheat – one of the most important ingredients for making pastries, breads, gateaux, biscuits and pies.

STONEGROUND FLOUR: This is simply a flour that has been finely ground between two large stone wheels in the old-fashioned way, which gives it a finer texture and a slightly better flavour. It can be used to make shortcrust pastry, brioches and bread dough.

FINE FLOUR: Best for making puff pastry and brioches.

SELF-RAISING FLOUR: This flour contains 3% baking powder and is good for making light airy cakes, biscuits, fruit cakes and pound cake.

CAKE FLOUR: Specially treated to prevent lumps from forming.

Corn flour ▶ Used in some regional French and exotic recipes.

Buckwheat flour ▶ A strong-flavoured flour with a speckled appearance – light brown in colour, it is used for some regional French desserts, such as Breton crêpes.

Starch ▶ Potato flour or cornflour. Cornflour, a fine white starch extracted from the maize kernel is an excellent thickening agent. Potato starch is a pure starch obtained from soaking potatoes in water. It is a very fine, white powder. Potato flour is useful as a thickening agent. Although pastry made with either of these flours is extremely light, it lacks cohesion. That is why some recipes use half cornflour or potato flour and half wheat flour. When using to thicken, dissolve these flours in cold liquid (milk or water) before adding to hot liquids for best results. Simmering or boiling liquid thickens after a few seconds.

Semolina ▶ Fine, medium or coarse ground, this is made of dried wheat by a special milling process. However, some recipes call for the same ingredient made from rice or corn, which is then called 'meal' instead. The word 'semolina' used on its own means wheat semolina. Fine semolina is used for making some heavy fruit sponge puddings and cream desserts. To use, always sprinkle into the boiling liquid. It is also used in the bottom of tarts for soaking up the juice from particularly juicy fruit as it absorbs liquid without causing the pastry to soften. Coarse semolina is also known as couscous which has been rolled, dampened and coated with finer wheat flour and is used in many savoury dishes.

Tapioca ▶ Extracted from cassava or manioc roots, this is useful for making cream desserts, thick light creamy sauces, gateaux and thick sponge puddings. It binds and thickens mixtures whilst making them smoother. Sprinkle onto the boiling liquid while stirring with a wooden spoon for 2 to 5 minutes Sweeten only when cooked.

Rice ▶ High in energy in comparison with its volume, rice is easily digested. It undergoes a variety of processes – including bleaching, glazing and polishing... – before it is sold. Rice comes in various forms.

POLISHED WHITE RICE: (American long-grain rice) The most common rice used in cooking. It is a good all-rounder rice and used in both sweet and savoury dishes. All of the outer husk has been removed. This rice should be washed, but not left to soak, before it is cooked, and then rinsed after cooking.

CONVERTED RICE: (par-boiled rice) This is a long-grain rice that has been partially steam-cooked so it retains some of its vitamins and mineral salts from the steaming process. It should not be washed before or after cooking.

Sugar

Cream

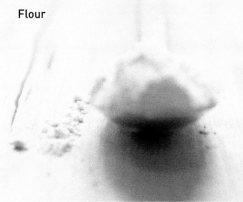

Flour

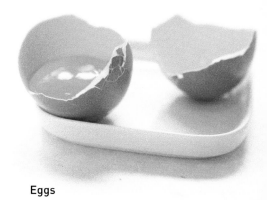

Eggs

Whether white or brown, rice of this kind never sticks.

SHORT-GRAIN RICE: These grains absorb up to five times their weight in liquid and release starch during cooking to create a creamy mixture. For sweet dishes use pudding rice – a short-grain rice sold specifically for rice pudding. Wash and blanch for a few minutes in boiling water before cooking in milk.

Eggs

Indispensable in many recipes. Yolks are used to bind pastry as well as creams. Beaten egg whites are added to mixtures to lighten them. They are also used in specific recipes such as meringues, floating island etc...

Choosing eggs

• A fresh egg looks shiny and velvety. When shaken, it feels full. On breaking, the yolk remains whole and round.
• An egg that has been laid the same day remains at the bottom when placed in a bowl filled with salt water. When the egg is a few days old, the larger end, which contains a pocket of air, rises to the surface.
• Variations in shell and yolk colour have no bearing on the quality of the egg.
• Eggs weighing 60–65g (medium size) are the best size to use for making desserts, cakes and pastries.
• Use particularly fresh eggs for uncooked and partially cooked mixtures.

Cooking with eggs

• Always break each egg separately before adding it to the main bowl. If an egg is bad, this prevents it spoiling the others.
• Avoid contact with silver teaspoon or other silverware.
• Eggshells are porous so eggs can take on the flavour of things kept nearby: avoid storing beside strong smelling foods (melons, onions, pineapple, etc.).
• Broken eggs do not keep as the white becomes toxic fairly quickly. They should either be used at once or frozen.

Fats

Butter ▸ Whether pasteurised or fresh, the most important thing is to ensure the butter is not old. Butter that is turning rancid gives a nasty taste. Salted butter, great for other uses, should be avoided in baking, except in some recipes that specify it.

Vegetable margarine and fat ▸ Made from oils extracted from vegetables, their uses are the same as for butter but they can endure higher temperatures. When frying beignets to serve hot, use solid vegetable fat/lard. However, if they are to be eaten cold, use oil as the fat solidifies when cold.

Oil ▸ Groundnut oil, made from peanuts, is the most commonly used for making desserts but some regional dishes specify other oils, such as olive or walnut oil. A spoonful of oil added to the pancake mix prevents it sticking and helps crisp the pancakes. Take care not to let oil burn. Watch carefully and filter after frying – it can be used several times before being renewed.

Raising agents

Stiffly beaten egg whites are used to make some mixtures rise, others use yeast or baking powder (see p. 63).

Baker's yeast ▸ Also known as brewer's yeast, this is made of microscopic fungi that react with humidity and warmth and cause flour to ferment and give off carbon dioxide. The gas bubbles are captured by the elastic dough and as they swell, cause it to rise. Fresh yeast is sold by weight and can be obtained from most bakers or the confectionary counters in some supermarkets. It should be used within one day. Dried yeast is available in 7g sachets. Yeast is sold in a stabilised state (in small packaged cubes) that can be stored in the freezer if they are not all used. Dried yeast can be

substituted for fresh yeast in recipes, but only half the amount should be used as it is more concentrated. Brewer's yeast which is slightly liquid is only really used in the production of beer or ale.

Baking powder ▸ A raising agent made up of cream of tartar and bicarbonate of soda mixed with a flour or starch. Generally, to use plain flour as a replacement for self-raising flour, add 4 level teaspoons of baking powder to each 8oz/225g of flour.

Gelatine

Helps thicken custard and fruit coulis, thereby enabling all sorts of creamy desserts to set. It comes in either a powdered form or translucent leaves. The leaves should be softened first in cold water, then dissolved in a warm liquid over a very low heat before adding to your mixture. When using powdered gelatine, add directly into the hot mixture. To make a gelatine-based dessert easier to remove from their moulds once set, pass the mould under cold water before filling it with the recipe mixture (without wiping it dry) and after the desserts is set, simply dip the mould in warm water for 30 seconds before turning the dessert out onto a serving plate.

Fruits

They are used in a variety of forms to decorate all sorts of cakes and desserts.

Fresh fruit ▸ This is always better and less expensive when it is in season. Remove the stones of any fruit used to make a dessert. Cherries are the only exception as their stones add a better flavour to clafoutis.
Take care to select the right kind of fruits for the dessert you are making.
FRUIT SALADS: Choose ripe flavourful fruit.
COMPOTES: You can used unripene or overripe fruits.
FLAMBÉEING: Select fruits with firm flesh.

TARTS: Delicate fruits should always be used raw and placed on cooked pastry. As a rule, only fruits with low water content can be cooked on uncooked pastry.

Chestnuts ▸ Use as they are, grilled or puréed for cakes and creams. Use tinned chestnut purée to make lovely ice creams and fillings for cakes. Select healthy-looking heavy nuts that have no staining or holes.

Almonds ▸ Fresh, green almonds are on sale from June to September; dried almonds can be found in various forms all year round. Shelled, they can be used to make pralines and nougat, and to decorate cakes; they are used sliced, chopped or ground in many recipes. Almonds turn rancid fairly quickly. Store in a sealed container in a dry place and use as soon as possible. Bitter almonds are used to flavour some creams, but should be used in moderation as they have a strong taste.

Walnuts ▸ Available fresh in August and September. The kernels, whole, halved or in pieces, are used to decorate gateaux and in cake mixtures. They may be crushed and added to fruit salads.
Walnuts go off quickly – store in a sealed container in a dry place and use as soon as possible.

Hazelnuts ▸ The nuts shouldn't have holes, which suggests worms. The nuts shouldn't rattle in their shells or they are old and probably rancid. Hazelnuts go off quickly, store in a sealed container in a dry place and use quickly. They are used in making praline. Roasted and crushed, they are used for decoration and in some recipes, in place of flour.

Pine nuts ▸ Also known as pine kernels, are used to decorate biscuits and gateaux.

Coconut ▸ The flesh makes delicious small cakes. When making floating islands add to the beaten egg whites for a delicate flavour.

Dried or dehydrated fruit ▸ Apricots, plums, pears, apples and peaches can be used to make compotes when fresh fruit is not available: soak and cook in water or slightly sweetened tea. Raisins and currants macerated in alcohol can be used with candied fruits to decorate fruit cakes, brioches and tarts.

Conserved fruit in tins or jars ▸ In syrup, they may be eaten as they are or used in a recipe. The syrup can also be used to soak the biscuits for a charlotte. In their own juices, they can be used to garnish tarts and make compotes.

Frozen fruit ▸ Some fruits freeze better than others. Frozen raspberries go well with fromage frais or fromage blanc, in fruit salads, ice creams, in charlottes and may be used whole to decorate gateaux. Frozen strawberries, on the other hand, hold their water content and are not as easily used whole. Use puréed in sauces, fillings and compotes. Blueberries freeze well and are great for making tarts. Defrost in the fridge before using.

Candied and preserved fruits ▸
These are used in classic recipes such as fruit cakes, rice puddings, ice cream bombes, Charlottes and other set puddings made using cake or bread to line the bowl, flavoured creams and rum babas. Store in a cool dry place in a sealed glass jar or plastic container.

Jams and jellies ▸ Jams are used to make creamy puddings, charlottes, Swiss rolls and to fill brioches, pancakes and sponges.
Jellies are sieved jams, often with a little sugar syrup added, and are used in a thin layer to cover the top of gateaux and tarts.

Butter

Baking powder

Leaf gelatine

Walnuts

Condiments and flavourings

These add character to a dessert. A recipe can be completely transformed by using a different flavouring.

Salt

Indispensable in most sweet recipes. A pinch (2g) is usually added.

Caramel

Frequently used in baking and to flavour desserts. It can be bought as a liquid flavouring if you don't want to make it yourself (see p. 16).

Alcohol

Used to add flavour to many desserts, pastries, creams, syrups and fruit-based sweets, for soaking rum babas and savarins, and to flambé pancakes and fruits such as bananas.
Use the more flavoursome types: rum, kirsch, brandy, armagnac, fruit eau de vie, anisette, orange liqueur…
Some alcohols contain synthetic flavourings, often unrelated to the name of the alcohol. Avoid these. Use orange or lemon zest instead.
Use sugar syrup flavoured with rum to infuse a baba.
For adding alcohol to a cream mixture, never add to the milk nor cook with the syrup. Always add at the end when the cream is cool or cold.
To flambé a dessert, warm the alcohol in a small pan taking care not to let it boil. Sprinkle caster sugar over the dessert, pour on the alcohol, tip the pan so that the alcohol runs to the side of the pan and carefully set alight, then stand back and allow the flames to naturally subside.

Fruit juice

Can be used fresh, tinned or in a carton to flavour creams and fruit salads. Add just before serving.

Orange flower water

This highly scented, delicate flavouring can be used to aromatise compotes, crêpes and pancakes, beignets, creams and egg mixtures. Use sparingly.

Spices

Cinnamon ▶ Used to flavour syrups, compotes, apple and almond cakes and gateaux.
It is sold powdered and in sticks that may be chopped up. Add to the liquid before boiling.
Cinnamon from Sri Lanka has a sweet floral flavour and is preferable to that from China, which is spicier.

Vanilla ▶ This is the fruit of an orchid from tropical forests. The best vanilla comes from Madagascar. This comes in dark brown pods whose pulp and seeds have a highly scented flavour. Half a pod, split lengthways in two is enough to flavour 1 litre/1¾ pints of milk. After infusing in hot liquid, rub the back of a knife or spoon down the inside of the pod to dislodge the tiny black seeds that contain vanilla's aromatic flavouring. Naturally flavoured vanilla sugar is also available, but should not be confused with synthetic vanilla sugar. You can make your own vanilla sugar by placing a pod with 50g/2oz sugar in a sealed jar. Natural vanilla can also be bought in a powdered or liquid form and may be added to creamy desserts using 1 tbsp per 1 litre/1¾ pints cream.

Chocolate

Chocolate is produced from the beans of the cocoa tree. Generally, the higher the cocoa solids content, the more intense the flavour. Bitter chocolate contains on average about 75% cocoa solids and is as its name suggest 'bitter' because no extra sugar has been added, giving it an incredibly rich flavour. Plain chocolate contains anywhere between 30–60% cocoa solids, depending on the quality. White chocolate derives its flavour from cocoa butter and is high in fat and sugar. This chocolate should be melted with care. Chocolate should be stored tightly wrapped in a cool, dry place, away from foods with strong flavours or aromas. Incorrectly stored it will form a whitish bloom and, although still edible, the chocolate is not as attractive and will not perform as well when it is cooked.
To flavour a liquid, add chocolate to it, using 125g/4½oz per 1 litre/1¾ pints.
You can make chocolate curls by spreading melted chocolate onto a clean smooth work surface such as marble. When only just set, push a clean round-bladed knife across the surface of the chocolate at a 25° angle until it curls back on itself. If the chocolate breaks, it has become too cool and should be left at room temperature to soften slightly before trying again.
For baking, only use chocolate containing 40% cocoa solids or more.

Coffee

Used to flavour and colour creams, ice creams and icing. Used either as coffee extract, as crushed beans added to the liquid and filtered later, or as a very strong coffee (6 tbsp ground coffee to 250ml/9fl oz water).
Instant coffee also gives a good flavour and a tablespoon quickly dissolves in just a few drops of hot water. Cool and use as coffee extract.

Praline

Used to flavour creams and ice creams. You can add crushed or powdered praline to a cooked cream. Store in sealed container.

Zest

This is the name given to the rind of citrus fruits that have been thinly peeled without removing the white pith, which has a bitter taste.
Citrus zest is exceptionally useful for flavouring desserts. When baking, choose unwaxed fruits. They need to be carefully washed, brushed and dried before use.
To flavour creams, boil the zest in the cream and remove after cooking.

Equipment

Moulds

Wooden spatula

Nowadays there is no limit to the types of baking tools and equipment available. However, it is not necessary to have a lot of specialist equipment to make a good dessert: the minimum in accessories (tins and moulds, a few essential tools) will ensure success.

Measuring instruments

MEASURING JUG OR GLASS: Essential for measuring both liquids and powders.
SCALES: Designed to fit on the wall or sit on a worktop, they can measure ingredients weighing 0–3kg/0–7lb.

Equipment used when preparing ingredients

ROLLING PIN: Usually made of wood; however, it can also be made of glass, plastic or even marble. Remember to flour the pin before use to avoid the dough sticking to it, and wash it carefully after use.

MIXING BOWLS: Bowls with a 20–25cm/ 8–10in diameter are easiest to use. Choose either metal or glass with a rounded shape and a slightly flattened base. This makes whisking easier than a flat-bottomed basin.
SPATULAS AND WOODEN SPOONS: Indispensable when making sponge mixtures or custards.
FINE SIEVE: In baking this is used to sift flour, as well as to filter sauces and coulis to remove lumps and seeds.
JUICER: Manually operated one in glass, stainless steel or plastic is ample for extracting citrus juices. Wooden implements which you insert directly into the fruit are also very useful.
GRATERS: You will need a coarse grater for chocolate and a fine one for orange and lemon zests.
ELECTRIC BEATER: This takes all the hard work out of beating when whisking egg whites or making cake mixtures.

Other accessories

FLOUR SIFTER: A cylindrical tin with a handle mechanism, which activates a lever that pushes the flour back and forth over the sieve in the bottom.
PALETTE KNIFE: Useful for getting a cake out of a tin and for smoothing the top of creams and toppings.
PASTRY BRUSH: Handy for buttering tins, brushing the top of pastry and for sticking down the edges of turnovers. Buy a flat silk brush, about 2.5cm/1in wide. Watch out – do not dip into liquids that are too hot or they will burn.
APPLE CORER: A useful tool of removing apple cores and all the pips without destroying the shape of the apple. Can also be used on pears.
NUTCRACKER: Select a solid cracker of a classical design.

Tins and moulds

Select the best material for your needs ▸ Cake moulds are mainly made of tin and some come with a non-stick surface.

Terra cotta and ceramic moulds are good for flans, clafoutis and gugelhupf. Ovenproof porcelain can be served at the table and is recommended for desserts and gateaux that are too delicate to remove without damaging. Pyrex glass dishes enable you to watch the cooking; they need to have a fairly thick base to conduct the heat evenly. Flexible silicone rubber moulds are frequently used today. Silicone is a very flexible material that withstands temperatures from -40°C–250°C and can be used in freezers, ovens and microwaves. Always be place on a rack, never on a tray. Especially useful for making small cakes.

Special moulds and tins

TART OR FLAN TINS: To make a tart that serves eight, you will need a 28cm/11in tin, a 24–26cm/9½–10in tin serves six, and a 20cm/8in tin serves four.
DEEP SANDWICH TINS: Used for Genoese sponges, composed puddings, pound cakes and clafoutis. The most frequently used size is 20cm/8in.
LOAF TIN: Rectangular in shape, this has high sides and is used for certain types of cake.
SAVARIN AND BABA MOULD: This ring mould is can also be used for cakes and creamy puddings.
CHARLOTTE MOULD: Used for cream-based desserts, crème caramels, some composed puddings and charlottes. A 16cm/6½in charlotte mould serves six to eight.
SOUFFLÉ MOULD: Can be made either of ovenproof porcelain or glass.
SPECIALIST MOULDS: There are also large moulds, individual moulds, brioche tins, gugelhupf moulds, fluted moulds, tins for making Madeleines or other small cakes, deep tins in novelty shapes such as hearts or fishes, tiny petit-fours tins that are even smaller than individual tins, as well as ice cream moulds that enable you to create unusual, entertaining and decorative presentations.

Tips and Tricks

Preparation

Softening the butter ▶ Take the butter out of the fridge an hour before starting to make the recipe. Cut into small squares and soften using a spatula or fork, or beating it with an electric beater. Avoid placing the butter near a source of heat. If you need melted butter, put it into the mould (non-metallic) and place in the oven while it is preheating, or microwave for 30 seconds. By doing this you will at the same time grease the mould. Don't forget to take the butter out of the oven as soon as it has melted.

Greasing a tin or mould ▶ There are several ways of doing this.
• Soften a small lump of butter and baste the tin using a pastry brush.
• Place the mould in the oven as it preheats and then quickly grease the hot tin, using a small knob of butter on the end of a fork.
• Use the butter paper: rub the tin or mould with the buttery side of the wrapping.
• Use margarine: place a knob on a piece of kitchen paper and rub it over the tin.
• Oil the bottom of the tin using a pastry brush.
If you are using one of the flexible silicone or glass mould that are suitable for both traditional and microwave ovens you won't need to grease it. Your cake or dessert will come out easily and whole, with a smooth, shining surface.

Flouring a tin or mould ▶ Tip a small amount of flour into the buttered or unbuttered tin, depending on the recipe. Tilt the tin slightly backwards and forewords to coat every part of it evenly, especially the corners, then tip out any excess.

Sugaring a tin or mould ▶ Coat in the same way as for flour, preferably using a buttered tin.

Lining a tin with baking paper ▶ In most cakes it is necessary to line the base and or sides of the tin with greaseproof paper or non-stick baking parchment. The latter is used for cake that is more likely to stick, such as meringue based cakes or roulades.
To LINE SQUARE TINS: Cut a square of paper the same size as the base. Cut strips 2cm/¾in wider than the depth of the tin. Snip the bottom edge at 1cm/½in intervals and about 1cm/½in deep, and use to line the sides of the tin, making sure the corners are neat. Cover with the square of paper.
To LINE A ROUND TIN: This is done in the same method, using one length of paper to line the side of the tin.
To LINE A LOAF TIN: Cut a strip of paper, the length of the tin base and wide enough to cover both the base and long sides – press into position. Then cut another strip of paper, the width of the tin base and long enough to cover the base and ends of the tin. Press the paper into position and fold over any overhanging paper.
To LINE A RECTANGULAR SWISS ROLL TIN: Cut a rectangle of paper 5cm/2in wider and longer than the tin and press into the tin. Cut the paper at the corners and fold neatly to fit.

Using a bain-marie ▶ A bain-marie is used for cooking and melting. One container is placed inside another, which is full of water that is kept at a steady simmer.

Making successful pastry in very hot weather ▶ Try to ensure that all the ingredients are about the same temperature: cool but not cold. Keep your hands cool by passing them under cold water from time to time. Place the pastry in the fridge between the different stages.

Melting chocolate ▶ Break the chocolate into small pieces and place them together with the water or milk, (depending on the recipe) in a bowl in the hot oven doorway, in a bain-marie or over a very gentle low heat, using a diffusing plate. Chocolate has melted when a knife slides into the pieces. If heated for too long, it turns granulated. 50g/2oz chocolate takes 1½ minutes on low power in the microwave.
For ganache, chop the chocolate finely and place in a mixing bowl. Bring the cream to the boil and pour over the chocolate, leaving for a few minutes before stirring, the chocolate will melt and thicken the cream slightly.

Adding egg whites ▶ Start by gently mixing a tablespoon of the beaten egg whites into the mixture, then add the rest in one go. Gently fold them in with a metal spoon by lifting the mixture to cover the whites and folding in, using a figure-of-eight motion. Never stir vigourously – you will knock all the air out of the mixture.

Sifting flour ▶ If you don't have a flour sifter, put the flour into a fine sieve and place over a bowl or above the worktop. Lightly tap the handle of the sieve, rather than shaking it to ensure that the flour doesn't go everywhere.

Cooking in the oven

To bake well, you have to get to know your oven. Always turn the oven on 10–15 minutes before putting in your gateau, except for fan ovens that do not need preheating.

Oven temperatures:
Gas ¼ = 110°C/fan oven 90°C
Gas ½ = 130°C/fan oven 100°C
Gas 1 = 140°C/fan oven 120°C
Gas 2 = 150°C/Fan oven 130°C
Gas 3 = 170°C/fan oven 150°C
Gas 4 = 180°C/fan oven 160°C
Gas 5 = 190°C/fan oven 170°C
Gas 6 = 200°C/fan oven 180°C
Gas 7 = 220°C/fan oven 200°C
Gas 8 = 230°C/fan oven 210°C
Gas 9 = 240°C/fan oven 220°C

Placing a cake or gateau into the oven

▸ Recipes that use egg whites, as well as mixtures that rise or have risen, should be placed on a shelf about 10cm/4in above the floor of the oven. Others can be placed in the middle of the oven, except if you want to achieve a more caramelised effect (in which case, place nearer the top). In a fan-assisted oven (which has a uniform temperature), cakes and gateaux can be cooked in any position. However, we would recommend the centre of the oven for the best results.

Deciding on cooking time for different-sized cakes

▸ Small cakes should be placed near the top of the oven at a higher temperature for a much shorter time than large cakes and gateaux.

If you double the quantities in a recipe, do not double the cooking time but add on about a third; and if that is the case, also lower the temperature just a fraction.

Stopping a cake or gateau from going brown too quickly

▸ Cover the top with baking paper.

Cooking sugar and caramel

Sugar is a wonderful resource in cooking, and in baking or preparing desserts; its use varies according to how it is cooked.

Equipment ▸ There are a number of specialist tools that can help you to succeed. The most useful, and the only one you absolutely need when working with caramel is the sugar thermometer. For other methods see below.

• SUGAR OR CONFECTIONERY THERMOMETERS: Heavy-duty thermometers mounted onto copper brackets or in little steel wire cages to protect the thermometer – they can be plunged directly into the caramel and will tell you whether the caramel is at the right stage for the purpose you are intending.

Caramel is the final stage when the sugar changes rapidly in colour, from translucent golden to deep brown – you need to keep an eye on it at each stage! When cleaning a thermometer, never plunge into cold water immediately after it has been in the syrup. Use hot water instead and leave to soak until the caramel has melted.

Spun sugar caramel ▸ To make spun sugar caramel, it is best to use sugar lumps. This form of pure sugar is less likely to crystallise on account of some impurity, which makes it unusable.

Ingredients :
200g/7oz white sugar lumps
85ml/3fl oz water
1 tsp vinegar or lemon juice

Cooking ▸ Put the sugar lumps, water and vinegar (or lemon juice) into a clean heavy-bottomed pan made of stainless steel or copper. Place on a low heat. Do not stir but shake the pan a couple of times to ensure an even distribution of heat as the sugar melts. As soon as the sugar comes to the boil, wash down the inside of the pan with a pastry brush dipped in cold water. Add the sugar thermometer and cook until the sugar reaches 155°C/311°F. Take the pan off the heat and leave the sugar to cool for 3 minutes before using.

Cooking caramel without themometer to the right stage ▸ Caramel can also be made by hand, by dropping small teaspoonfuls into cold water and examining the result. This method is far less accurate. Here are the main terms and definitions in French and English as used by professional confectionery cooks:

NAPPÉ [coating; 100°C/212°F – 1,240]: The syrup is just coming to the boil, has become transparent, and forms a coating on the surface of a skimmer. USES: fruits in syrup.

Baking paper

Work with cool hands in heat

Grated chocolate

Sugaring a tin or mould

PETIT FILET (SMALL THREAD; 101°C/214°F – 1,251]: When the sugar begins to boil, plunge thumb and forefinger into a bowl of cold water and very quickly lift up a little syrup: it forms a thin 2–3mm/⅛in strand between your fingers. USES: marzipan.

GRAND FILET OR LISSÉ (LARGE THREAD; 102–103°C/215–217°F – 1,262]: The strand is about 5mm/⅛in long and less fragile than at the previous stage. USES: buttercream.

PETIT PERLÉ [SMALL PEARL; 104-105°C/219-221°F – 1,296]: Large round bubbles form on the surface of the syrup, the string formed between the fingers is strong when you move your fingers apart. USES: touron.

GRAND PERLÉ OR SOUFFLÉ [LARGE PEARL; 107°C/225°F – 1,319]: Solid bubbles form when you blow across the skimmer after dipping in the syrup. The string stretches to about 2cm/1in between your fingers without breaking. USES: syrup for making jam, for glacé chestnuts and cherries.

PETIT BOULÉ [SOFT BALL; 109–116°C/228–241°F – 1,344]: A small amount of syrup taken from the pan with a spoon and dropped into a bowl of cold water, will form a soft pliable ball. USES: jams.

GROS BOULÉ [HARD BALL; 120–126°C/248–259°F – 1,357]: Use the previous method to check this stage. The ball is still pliable but it is firmer. USES: fondant, nougat, soft caramel, and Italian (soft) meringue.

PETIT CASSÉ [SOFT OR SMALL CRACK; 129–133°C/264–271°F – 1,439]: Use the same method as the previous two stages to check this: the ball is now hard and sticky. USES: marzipan.

GRAND CASSÉ [HARD CRACK; 145–150°C/293–302°F – 1,452]: When the syrup is tipped from the spoon into ice-cold water, the drop solidifies and becomes breakable, like glass. It doesn't stick and is still colourless. Before coating fruits wait until the sugar at the sides of the pan starts to turn pale yellow. USES: hard caramels, boiled sweets, pastilles, barley sugar, lollipops, spun sugar, stuffed fruits, coating fruits.

CLEAR CARAMEL [151-160°C/304–320°F – 1,466]: The sugar turns yellow. USES: caramelising choux pastry and fruits, nougatine, crème caramel.

DARK CARAMEL [161-170°C/321–338°F – 1,480]: The sugar takes on a darker colour. Above 190°C it blackens, gives off an acrid smoke and burns. USES: flavouring, caramel for colouring.

Using caramel
Caramel is used in various ways, depending on its colour and cooking.
PALE CARAMEL: Great for icing petit fours. Remove from the heat as soon as the edges start to take on colour.
CLEAR PALE GOLD CARAMEL: Used to pour over cream filled choux pastries and to build Croquembouche.
GOLDEN CARAMEL: Used for coating moulds for certain desserts, for preparing rice puddings and crème caramel.
BROWN CARAMEL: Its bitter flavour is not used in desserts.

Successfully making caramel
• Do not use implements to mix or stir the caramel. Keep a close eye on the cooking and shake the pan from time to time to diffuse the heat.
• Don't forget to sweeten caramel mixtures as cooking removes the sweetness from sugar. Consider using liquid caramel, which is readily available in shops, as a topping for gateaux and ice creams.

• To ensure caramel stays liquid for long enough, as for example when using to cover individual fruits or choux pastries, add half a teaspoon of vinegar or a drizzle of lemon juice for each 100g/4oz sugar.

Coating a mould or tin with caramel
OFF THE HOB: When the mould cannot go on top of the stove, heat the sugar (100g/4oz sugar with 3 tablespoons water) in a small pan. At the same time, warm the empty mould in the oven to prevent the caramel setting immediately on contact. When the caramel is ready, pour it into the mould and tilt gently until the mould is completely coated (make sure you use oven gloves to hold the mould as this will be extremely hot and so will the caramel).

ON THE HOB: You will need about 80g/3¼oz sugar lumps for a 20cm/8in pie tin. Moisten the sugar lumps and place them in the tin on a medium heat and keep a close eye. As soon as the sugar reaches the desired colour (pale golden or deep golden depending on the recipe), use a cloth or oven gloves to remove the tin from the heat and tip so that the caramel completely covers it. Leave the tin upright to cool. This will avoid a deposit forming in the bottom of the tin.
TO MICROWAVE: Use a microwave mould and proceed as for caramelising on top of the hob. Follow the instructions given in microwave manual.

"Cooling down" caramel ▶ Use 85g/3¼oz sugar to 500ml/18fl oz milk. When the caramel starts to turn a deep russet colour, stop cooking instantly by quickly tipping in half a glass of hot water (watch out for the steam). Dissolve by stirring and use this thick syrup to flavour milk.

Caramel-flavoured milk ▶ Never add hot caramel directly to milk! Instead, always "cool the caramel down first" (see above) with a little water.

Decorating creamy desserts with caramel ▸ Make a pale gold caramel and drizzle onto desserts as soon as it reaches the desired colour.

Making glacé fruits ▸ Make a pale gold caramel (one and a half sugar lumps for each fruit).
Thread the fruits onto wooden skewers, brochettes or toothpicks and dip them in turn into the caramel. Make sure you don't touch the hot caramel. Leave on the skewers to cool over an empty bowl or mould that acts as a support.

Caramelising choux pastries ▸ Make a pale gold caramel with vinegar in a small pan (use about one and a half sugar lumps for each choux ball). Dip each ball into the caramel, one by one, holding by the base. Place on a wire rack to cool.

Taking a dessert out of a mould or tin

Removing a gateau from a tin ▸ Some gateaux need to be taken out of their tins as soon as they come out of the oven, others when they have cooled a little, depending on the recipe.
Place the wire cooling rack on top of the tin, ensuring your hands are properly protected so that you don't burn yourself, and quickly turn both the tin and the rack over together in one smooth movement. Never use a sharp metal knife to dislodge the gateau as you risk scratching and damaging the tin.
If you should need to use an implement to help unstick a gateau, use a flat, flexible knife or spatula. If you still can't get the gateau out in spite of all this, place a damp tea towel or cloth on the bottom of the upturned tin and wait for 1 to 2 minutes.

Removing assembled desserts, charlottes or crème caramels ▸
Never turn the mould upside down onto a plate. Always place the serving plate or dish on top of the mould and then turn both over together in one movement and delicately lift off the mould. You should be able to feel the mixture drop onto the plate – if it doesn't, give the plate and mould a gently shake until the mixture drops.

Taking ice cream out of a mould ▸
Sit the mould in cold water then proceed as above.

To remove a gateau from a metal baking sheet or tray ▸ Slip a flexible spatula or metal knife under the gateau and use it to slide the gateau onto the cooling rack. Avoid using a knife that might mark the baking sheet. To prevent the gateau sticking, line the baking tray with baking paper before setting the cake on it. Never place cakes or gateaux on top of one another while cooling on the rack.

Successfully assembling a dessert

Slicing a cake into layers without breaking ▸ Place the gateau on a flat surface. Slice it horozontally, using a sharpened long serrated knife or bread knife or an electric knife. Handle each layer with care.

Keeping crêpes and pancakes warm
In a bain-marie: Pile the sugared crêpes onto a plate and place on top of a pan, filled two-thirds with simmering water. Cover with aluminium foil or a plate.

In a pan: This method is useful for ready-made crêpes, bought in a packet. Reheat them one by one with a small lump of butter in a pan set on a low heat. If they are difficult to unstick from each other, place for a few minutes on a plate on top of a pan of boiling water.

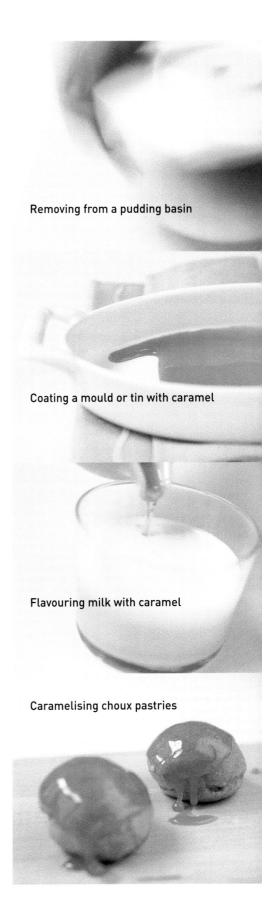

Removing from a pudding basin

Coating a mould or tin with caramel

Flavouring milk with caramel

Caramelising choux pastries

IN THE OVEN: Wrap plain crêpes in aluminium foil and place them in the oven for 10 to 15 minutes on a very low heat. The filling in stuffed crêpes stops them from drying out – arrange them on a plate and reheat in a low oven without covering.

IN THE MICROWAVE: Wrap the creêpes in kitchen paper to prevent them from becoming soggy.

Defrosting a gateau ▸ It is best to take a cake out of the freezer about two hours before serving.

Taking ice cream out of the freezer ▸ Leave ice cream for 10 to 15 minutes at room temperature before eating, to fully appreciate the flavour and creaminess. All the ice cream should then be finished. If you wish to keep some of it, cut off what you need while it is still hard and return the rest to the freezer without delay.

Slicing ice cream ▸ Soak a knife for a few minutes in hot water before using.

Cutting a tart ▸ Never cut a tart in its tin, which will scratch. Always cut the tart from the edge to the middle so as not to break up the tart.

Using fruits for dessert

Peeling fresh peaches ▸ Place two or three peaches together in a sieve. Plunge them into boiling water for about 10 seconds if they are very ripe and 20 to 30 seconds for less ripe fruit. Freshen under cold water – the skin will slip off easily.

Coring apples and pears ▸ Remove apple cores before peeling the fruit: the protection of their skin stops them from breaking up. Use an apple corer to empty out whole apples. If you don't have one, use a small sharp knife. For pears that have been cut in half, use a

teaspoon or a tablespoon, depending on the size of the fruit.

Stopping fruit from turning brown ▸ Only use silver or stainless steel utensile. Rub or sprinkle cut fruits with lemon juice.

Washing delicate fruit ▸ Some fruits, such as strawberries and raspberries, are particularly delicate. In general, raspberries are never washed – gently rolling the berries over a damp cloth is usually sufficient.
Strawberries, on the other hand, should be washed to remove any soil by placing them in a sieve and rapidly passing them under cold running water. Do not soak in water.

Removing the flesh from a melon ▸ cut a small circle in the top with a sharp knife and use the side of a spoon to scoop out the flesh without breaking the skin. For an attractive presentation, make small balls from the flesh, using a melon baller.

Skinning sweet chestnuts ▸ To remove the skins more easily, make an incision in the rounded side of the chestnut, which goes through the tough outer skin and the soft inner husk below that. Plunge a few into boiling water and leave to soak for 5 minutes. Then peel off both skins at the same time.

Slicing a pineapple ▸ Cut off the leaves with 2–3cm/1–1½in of the top of the edible part, using a sharp knife with a long blade. Slice the unpeeled pineapple horizontally, using an electric or slightly serrated knife. Insert the tip of the knife between the outer skin and the flesh in each of the slices in turn and work round, cutting off the skin. To make nicely shaped fruit pieces, use a pastry cutter to remove the hard centre of the pineapple slices. You can also slice

a pineapple in two lengthways and then into as many slices as you wish, like a melon. Carefully remove the centre and separate the flesh from the skin. Cut the flesh into slices and stagger these in the shell, arranging them alternately on one side and the other.

Poaching fruit ▸ Make a light syrup, add lemon juice, lemon or orange zest and spices of your choice (star anise, vanilla, cinnamon, cloves...), or a few peppercorns.

Macerating dried fruit ▸ Pour an infusion of hot tea onto the dried fruit (plums, apricots, dates, figs...) and leave to cool. You can add a stick of cinnamon, a vanilla pod or a few cardamom seeds for flavour.

Making a red fruit coulis ▸ Strawberries and raspberries should be liquidised and then passed through a fine sieve to remove small seeds. Fruits without seeds are just liquidised. Add a little lemon juice.

Removing peel from citrus fruit ▸ To obtain fine slivers of citrus fruit zest, use a potato or vegetable peeler that pares off the rind but doesn't cut deep enough to include the bitter white pith. For finer zesting, use a special zester or cut tiny slivers off the peels. When adding zest to flavour a mixture, rub the fruit skin carefully on a very fine grater.

Decorative sweets
Decoration should complement a dessert; it is the final touch that sets it off. You can do this yourself by using a variety of multicoloured sweets, chocolate decorations, silver balls and other items that are readily available. Depending on the desired result, decorations can be made or prepared before or after cooking the dessert.
Before cooking ▸ To give tarts and other types of pastries and desserts a lovely golden colour and sheen, you

just need to brush the surface lightly with a mixture of egg yolk and water or sugar and milk.

Before cooking is finished ▶ To caramelise tarts and soufflés, sprinkle them with caster or granulated sugar. Fruit jelly, dried and candied fruits, and meringues can be added at the same time.

After cooking

DECORATING SMALL BISCUITS AND SHORTBREADS: Sprinkle caster sugar, icing sugar, demerara sugar or brown sugar over the biscuits. For small cakes and buns, use a decoration that reflects their flavour – choose, for example, grated chocolate, slivers of citrus zest or pieces of fruit and nuts (depending on the recipe).

DECORATING FESTIVE DESSERTS: Icing is suitable for decorating Genoese sponge cakes and pound cakes. Spread the icing over the cake or gateau when it has cooled. The icing can be flavoured with vanilla, lemon, orange, liqueur, coffee, chocolate, coconut or caramel.
The most spectacular type of icing is royal or white icing, made with icing sugar, egg white and a few drops of lemon juice.
You can also cover desserts with fondant. Buy it ready-made or make your own using a sugar syrup with 500g/1lb 2oz sugar lumps, 100ml/3½fl oz water and 15g/½oz liquid glucose and ½ teaspoon of vinegar or lemon juice.

TO ADD HEIGHT TO A FLAT GATEAU: Decorate the top by piping buttercream icing over it, using a piping bag.

SERVING WITH FRUIT SALADS, ICE CREAMS, CRÊPES AND MILK AND FRUIT PUDDINGS: Sauces and fruit coulis are precious allies as they are quick and easy to make. You can use apricots, red fruits,

oranges, chocolate, caramel and liqueurs. Serve in a little bowl and drizzle some over the dessert.

DECORATING CHILDREN'S BIRTHDAY CAKES: Marzipan is ideal as you can colour it and create all sorts of novelty shapes and decorations to suit the occasion. To cover a cake, first roll out the marzipan, using a rolling pin.

FROSTING ICE CREAM AND SORBET GLASSES: Pour granulated sugar into a glass container with a lid. Add a few drops of food colouring and shake thoroughly (coloured sugar is also available ready-made). Sprinkle onto one plate and put the juice of a fleshly squeezed lemon into another. Dip the rim of each glass in turn into the lemon juice and then in the sugar. Press down lightly and twist to ensure the rim is properly covered. Set the glass upright and leave to dry. To serve, take the sorbet or ice cream out a little earlier to soften. Make balls by using an ice cream scoop and divide between the prepared glasses.

Storing desserts

Storing leftover desserts ▶ Place in a sealed container in the fridge. Never keep desserts based on raw eggs for more than 24 hours.

Storing cooked cakes and gateaux ▶ Before storing cakes, make sure they have gone completely cold to prevent any moisture collecting. They should be kept in a sealed container, either a plastic box or a tin.

Storing ice cream ▶ Ice cream can be kept for up to 30 minutes at room temperature in insulated packaging, without opening; or for a few hours in its packaging in the fridge; or for up to half a day in a cool box; or for several months in the freezer. Retain the packaging if you need to transport the ice cream afterwards.

Red fruit coulis

Decorative sugar sweets and baubles

Macerating fruit

Canelle for removing zest from citrus fruit

[Shortcrust

p a s t r y]

The secret to a good sweet or savoury pie or tart is definitely the pastry. Shortcrust pastry is used for making individual tarts, pies, and turnovers. This type of pastry is easy to make. Success depends on your speed of execution and on using all the ingredients in the right proportions to each other. Despite what is often said, shortcrust pastry should not be kneaded for any length of time. Just mix the ingredients well together and add enough water to make pastry that it is neither too wet nor to dry.

Pastry recipe for a tart serving 6
(One 26cm/10½in tart)
200g/7oz flour
½ tsp fine salt
1 or 2 tbsp caster sugar, as preferred
100g/4oz butter
3–5 tbsp water

These proportions make about 225g/8oz shortcrust pastry, enough for around fifteen individual tartlets or one larger tart.
To make more or less shortcrust pastry always keep to the same proportions, remembering that the butter should weigh half the amount of the flour.

Some recipes in this chapter use slightly different ingredients to make shortcrust pastry. The proportions for the recipe are given in each case.

Preparation
Tip all the flour into a mixing bowl and make a well in the centre. Cut the butter into small pieces and place in the centre, together with the salt and sugar. Lightly mix everything together with the tips of your fingers to form a crumble. Gradually add the water to the mixture and bring it together to form a ball, without kneading: the pastry should be supple but not too soft. Set aside to rest and chill for at least 30 minutes.
Work the pastry: Use the palm of your hand to spread it out, helping it to stick together. Lightly flour the rolling pin and the worktop before lowering the pastry onto it. Do so gently, to avoid having to form a ball again. Only grease the tin, if the filling contains eggs, sugar and milk. Fold the pastry in four to make it easier to place in the tin, then open it up and press in lightly all round using your index fingers. Remove excess pastry using a knife against the top of the tin – or simply

run a rolling pin over the top and press again with your finger to lift the pastry just above the top of the tart tin.

Baking blind
Pastry cases for tarts or pie are often partially or completely cooked before a moist filling is added. This is called 'baking blind'. Simply prick the base of the pastry with a fork to prevent steam building up under the pastry base. Line the pastry case with greaseproof paper and then fill with dried beans or rice to prevent the sides from collapsing or the base from rising. Cook in a preheated oven Gas 7/220°C/fan oven 200°C on a preheated baking sheet for 10–12 minutes until the edges start to brown. Remove paper and beans or rice and return the tin to the oven for a further 5 minutes until crisp and golden.

Storing
Uncooked and unfilled, this pastry may be kept in a sealed container in the lower part of the fridge for 1–2 days. It can also be frozen, whether cooked or uncooked, garnished or not, in a ball or rolled flat. Once it has been cooked it should be eaten within 2 days.

Tarte Tatin ›

Serves 6 to 8
PREPARATION TIME: 30 minutes
COOKING TIME: 40–45 minutes plus
20 minutes resting time

FOR THE FILLING
100g/4oz butter
200g/7oz caster sugar
2 kg/4½lb apples
(golden delicious or other
dessert apples)

FOR THE SHORTCRUST PASTRY
50g/2oz caster sugar
200g/7oz flour
125g/4½oz butter cut
into small pieces
1 egg

Make the filling: cut the butter into slices and arrange in the bottom of a deep heavy-duty 24cm/9in sandwich tin or ovenproof pan. Sprinkle over the sugar to cover. Peel and quarter the apples. Arrange the apples (the outer curved part should be placed to touch the sugar) in concentric circles in the tin – they should completely cover the sugar and be packed snugly together.

Place the tin or pan on the gas hob on a medium heat for about 20 minutes keeping an eye on the bubbles and colour of the caramel, which should be pale gold.

Meanwhile, make the shortcrust pastry: mix the sugar and flour together and rub in the butter to form a fine breadcrumb-like mixture. Add the egg and stir to just combine. Make a ball and set aside to rest for 10 minutes.

Preheat oven to Gas 7/220°C/fan oven 200°C. Use a rolling pin to roll out the pastry to a circle slightly bigger than the tin, place on top of the apples, pushing any excess pastry down into the tin. Bake for 20–25 minutes until the pastry is risen and golden brown. When cooked, remove the tart from the oven and leave to cool for 10 minutes.

Place the warm tart on the heat for a few minutes – this will help to remove it from the tin. Place a serving plate over the tart and quickly turn both over in one smooth move (wear oven gloves to protect my hands – beware the caramel is hot so hold the plate and tin firmly together). Lift the tin off and serve warm or cold.

Sugar tart

Serves 6 to 8
PREPARATION TIME: 20 min
COOKING TIME: 40–45 minutes

60g/2½oz butter + a little
to grease the pie dish
330g/10½oz shortcrust pastry
150g/5oz caster sugar
2 tbsp vanilla sugar
30g/1¼oz flour
225ml/8fl oz single cream
1 egg
Juice ½ lemon
1 tbsp cognac
grated nutmeg

Preheat oven to Gas 4/180°C/fan oven 160°C.

Lightly butter a 26cm/10⅛in pie dish. Roll out the pastry on a lightly floured surface to 3mm/⅛in thick and place in the pie dish. Fold back the edges to form a rim. Chill while preparing the filling.

Mix together the caster sugar, vanilla sugar and flour in a bowl. Add the cream, egg, lemon juice and the cognac. Beat to form a smooth mixture and pour into the pastry case.

Arrange small knobs of butter over the surface and sprinkle with freshly grated nutmeg. Place in the middle of the oven and cook for 40–45 minutes or until the filling is set. Allow to cool and serve sprinkled with the remaining vanilla sugar.

Apricot custard tart

Serves 8

PREPARATION TIME: 20 minutes
COOKING TIME: 50 minutes

20g/¾oz butter
1 tbsp plain flour
330g/10½oz shortcrust pastry
1kg/2¼lb fresh apricots
2 medium eggs
100g/4oz demerara sugar
+ 1 tbsp
225ml/8fl oz thick crème fraîche

Preheat oven at Gas 6/ 200°C/fan oven 180°C.

Lightly butter and flour a 26cm/10½in pie tin with a removable base. Roll out the pastry on a lightly floured surface to 3mm/⅛in thick and use to line pie tin. Trim off any excess pastry. Prick the bottom of the pastry case with a fork. Fill with greaseproof paper and baking beans and bake blind for 10 minutes. Remove beans and paper and return to the oven for 5 minutes.

Meanwhile, wash and trim the apricots. Cut them in half and remove the stones. Arrange cut side down on the base of the pastry case.

Whisk the eggs with 100g/4oz of demerara sugar in a mixing bowl with an electric whisk until they form a creamy mousse (this should take about 7–8 minutes), continue beating and add the crème fraîche. Pour the mixture over the apricots and return to the oven for 25 minutes.

Sprinkle with the remaining demerara sugar and return to the oven for a further 15 minutes. Allow the tart to stand for 5 minutes in the tin before transferring onto a serving plate. Serve warm or cold.

COOK'S TIP

Use tinned or conserved apricots to make this recipe out of season. Drain well and sprinkle 60g/2½oz of ground almonds in the bottom of the pastry case before arranging the fruit: the almonds soak up the juices from the fruits as they cook.

Rhubarb tart with speculoos

Serves 6

PREPARATION TIME: 20 minutes
COOKING TIME: 45 minutes

1kg/2lb 4oz rhubarb
150g/5oz caster sugar
230g/1¼oz shortcrust pastry
125g/4½oz speculoos or plain lebkuchen biscuits
(about 17 biscuits)
30g/1¼oz butter,
cut into small pieces
2 tbsp demerara sugar
225ml/8fl oz double cream

Carefully clean, peel and slice the rhubarb stems, cutting into small pieces. Put in a pan with the caster sugar, cover with a lid and cook on a hot heat for 5 minutes, then uncover and continue cooking for a further 5 minutes until softened and pale pink. Let the mixture cool and then break up with a fork to make a compote. Drain.

Preheat oven to Gas 4/180°C/fan oven 160°C. Roll out the pastry on a lightly floured surface to 3mm/⅛in thick and use to line a 20cm/8in deep pie dish. Trim off any excess pastry. Prick the bottom of the pastry case with a fork. Fill with greaseproof paper and dried beans and bake blind for 10 minutes. Remove the beans and paper and return to the oven for 5 minutes.

Break up the biscuits and scatter over the base of the tart. Pour the rhubarb compote over and smooth the surface. Dot with knobs of butter and sprinkle with the demerara sugar. Place in the middle of the oven and cook for 35 minutes. Allow the tart to stand for 5 minutes in the tin before transferring onto a serving plate. Serve warm with double cream.

Custard flan

(see p. 21)

serves 8

PREPARATION TIME: 30 minutes
COOKING TIME: 40 minutes
plus resting time

SHORTCRUST PASTRY
150g/5oz flour
½ tsp salt
1 tsp caster sugar
75g/3oz butter
100ml/3¼fl oz water

CUSTARD CREAM
600ml/1pint milk
1 vanilla pod, split
4 eggs
150g/5oz caster sugar
70g/2¾ cornflour

Make the shortcrust pastry (see p. 21) and leave to rest for 20-30 minutes. Meanwhile, Pour the milk into a large pan, add the vanilla pod and bring to the boil. Cool slightly then remove the vanilla pod.

Preheat oven to 190°C/375°F (gas 5). Roll out the pastry on a lightly floured surafce and use to line and line a 24cm/9½in deep tin deep tin.

Beat the eggs and sugar together in a large mixing bowl until pale. Beat in the cornflour and pour over one third of the infused milk and whisk well to combine, then pour back into the pan with the milk and whisk well. Cook over a low heat stirring continuously until the mixture has thickened slightly and coats the back of a wooden spoon. Pour into the pastry case and bake for about 40 minutes. Leave the tart to cool before removing from the tin.

[Sablée

pastry]

Sablée pastry is a very delicate kind of shortcrust pastry. It has a fine, grainy texture, which is why it is called "sablée", meaning sandy. It is used to make small biscuits, tarts and tartlets. For easy success, you need to follow the method scrupulously.

The ingredients

These ingredients make about 250g/9oz sablée pastry, enough to make 30–40 x 8cm/3¼in shortbread biscuits or about 15 tartlets. To make a larger or smaller quantity, use the same proportions, bearing in mind that the butter and sugar should always both weigh the same amount for this pastry and that the flour should weigh as much as both combined.
To flavour the pastry, you can replace the lemon with other flavours, such as vanilla or rum.
Some recipes in this chapter use slightly different ingredients to make sablée pastry. The proportions for the recipe are given are given in each case.

Serves 6
(Makes one 26cm/10½in tart)
1 egg weighing 55g/2oz
125g/4½oz caster sugar
¼ tsp salt
250g/9oz flour
125g/4½oz butter
finely grated zest of 1 unwaxed lemon

The preparation

Beat the egg in a bowl. Add the sugar and salt and beat the mixture with a spatula until it forms a thick creamy mousse. Sieve the flour onto a piece of greaseproof paper and then add all at once to the mixture. Mix in, using the spatula. Lift the pastry with the tips of the fingers to form tiny crumbs. Add the butter to this "sand"-like mixture and rub in with the fingertips, then add the grated lemon zest. Place the pastry on the worktop. It shouldn't stick to your fingers. Make a ball. Flour the worktop and roll out the pastry. Place in the fridge for 1 hour to firm, especially in hot weather. Sablée pastry can easily be made using a kitchen chef mixer: just place all the ingredients in and let the machine do the hard work!

Cooking

Sablée pastry should be baked blind at a medium temperature, Gas 6/200°C/fan oven 180°C for 10 minutes. Remove biscuits from the oven when they start to turn pale golden. Remove from the baking tray immediately and place on a wire rack to cool. Do not overlap them. When making a tart, let it cool before removing from the tin, as the pastry is delicate when hot. When you cut out pastry using a pastry cutter, try to waste as little as possible. Use a spatula to lift each biscuit and place on a buttered baking tray. The biscuits don't rise during cooking.

Storing

Biscuits keep for 15 days in a sealed container. Tarts wrapped in cling film can be kept for 1–2 days in the fridge. Uncooked home-made pastry keeps for 24 hours in the lower part of the fridge or for 3–4 weeks in the freezer.

Fromage blanc gateau ▸

Serves 8 to 10
PREPARATION TIME: 40 minutes
COOKING TIME: 25 minutes plus
1 hour resting time

FOR THE SABLÉE PASTRY
1 medium egg
100g/4oz caster sugar
pinch salt
330g/10½oz flour
150g/5oz butter
zest of 1 lemon

FOR THE FILLING
500g/1lb 2oz fromage blanc
1 tbsp crème fraîche
150g/5oz caster sugar
½ tbsp vanilla sugar
1 tbsp flour
1 tbsp potato flour
finely grated zest of 1 lemon
6 medium eggs, separated

Make the sablée pastry **(following the preparation method on p. 27)** and leave to rest for 30 minutes. Preheat oven to Gas 6/200°C/fan oven 180°C. Roll out the pastry on a lightly floured surface to 3mm/⅛in thick and use to line a 26cm/10½in spring form cake tin with 4cm/½in sides. Prick the bottom with a fork and bake blind for 10 minutes. Remove the pastry case and increase the oven temperature to Gas 7/220°C/fan oven 200°C.

Beat the fromage blanc with an electric whisk until it is smooth and creamy. Whisk in the crème fraîche, caster sugar, vanilla sugar, flour, potato flour and lemon rind until well combined. Beat in the egg yolks.

Whisk the egg whites until stiff and gently fold into the mixture. Pour into the pastry case, it should only three quarters of the tin. Bake for 15 minutes, then reduce the oven temperature to

Gas 3/170°C/fan oven 140°C and continue cooking for a further 45 minutes. Half-way through, cooking cover the cake with baking paper to prevent it from going brown too quickly. When the gateau is ready, take out of the oven leave for 30 minutes to cool, then release the clip on the spring form tin and remove. Make sure the gateau has completely cooled before sliding off the base and onto a serving plate. Serve chilled.

Italian almond gateau

Serves 8 to 10
PREPARATION TIME: 30 minutes
COOKING TIME: 1 hour

SABLÉE PASTRY
2 egg yolks
120g/4½oz sugar
250g/9oz flour
120g/4½oz butter

FILLING
200g/7oz coarsely
ground almonds
200g/7oz caster sugar
100g/4oz butter,
plus extra for greasing

Make the sablée pastry **(following the preparation method on p. 27)**. Roll out the pastry on a lightly floured surface to 2mm thick then, using a knife, slice into very thin strips (like noodles or pasta). Mix the almonds and caster sugar together.

Preheat oven to Gas 2/150°C/fan oven 130°C. Generously butter a deep 22cm/8½in sandwich tin. Scatter some of the pastry 'noodles' over the base of the tin to just about cover. Scatter over some of the almond mixture. Dot with small pieces of butter on top. Repeat the process as many times as necessary, taking care to finish with the pastry 'noodles'. Bake for 1 hour. Allow to cool in the tin. Just before serving, run a flat-bladed knife around the edge of the tin and carefully transfer the gateau to a serving plate.

Raspberry tart gratinée

Serves 6 to 8
PREPARATION TIME: 35 minutes
COOKING TIME: 40–50 minutes
plus resting time

SABLÉE PASTRY
1 egg yolk
60g/2½oz caster sugar
125g/4½oz flour
60g/2½oz butter
1 tbsp milk

FILLING
1 egg white, lightly beaten
500g/1lb 2oz raspberries

FOR THE GRATIN
100g/4oz flour
150g/5oz caster sugar
75g/3oz butter
250ml/9fl oz crème fraîche or
double cream, to serve (optional)

Make the sablée pastry (following the method on p. 27) and leave to rest for 1 hour.

Preheat oven to Gas 6/200°C/fan oven 180°C. Roll out the pastry on a lightly floured surface and use to line a 24cm/9½in tart tin. Brush the bottom of the pastry with the egg white and bake blind for 10 minutes. Remove the paper and beans and return to the oven for 5 minutes. Increase the oven temperature to Gas 9/240°C/fan oven 220°C.

Scatter the raspberries into the pastry case. Mix together the flour and caster sugar. Cut the butter into small pieces and rub in, using the tips of your fingers, until the mixture resembles coarse breadcrumbs. Use to cover the raspberries. Place on a high shelf in the oven and bake for about 30–40 minutes, or until the gratin cooks to a lovely golden brown. Serve warm or cold, accompanied by crème fraîche or double cream.

Chocolate fondant tart ›

Serves 6 to 8
PREPARATION TIME: 40 minutes
COOKING TIME: 40 minutes
plus resting time

SABLÉE PASTRY WITH
CHOCOLATE CHIPS
1 medium egg
Pinch salt
125g/4½oz caster sugar
250g/9oz flour
125g/4½oz soft butter,
plus extra for greasing
50g/2oz chocolate chips

FILLING
400g/14oz rich dark chocolate
350ml/12fl oz crème fraîche
40g/1½oz caster sugar
2 medium eggs

DECORATION (OPTIONAL)
Icing sugar
Liqueur filled chocolate eggs

Make the sablée pastry: beat together the egg, salt and caster sugar in a mixing bowl until it forms a thick creamy mousse. Sift the flour and scatter over the mixture. Incorporate with a spatula, then rub the mixture with your fingertips, adding the butter gradually to form fine crumbs. When it is all thoroughly rubbed in, knead lightly and add the chocolate chips, making sure they are distributed evenly throughout. Make the pastry into a ball, wrap in cling film and chill for 1 hour in the fridge.

Preheat the oven to Gas 6/200°C/fan oven 180°C. Lightly butter a 26cm/10½in tart tin. Roll out the pastry on a lightly floured surface and use to line the tin. Trim off any excess pastry. Prick the base with a fork and bake blind for 10 minutes. Remove the paper and baking beans and return to the oven for 5 minutes. Remove and set aside. Lower the oven temperature to Gas 4/180°C/fan oven 160°C.

Make the filling: break the chocolate into small pieces, place in a bowl set over a pan of simmering water and heat gently until melted. Remove from the heat and beat in the crème fraîche and caster sugar until the sugar has dissolved and the mixture forms a smooth cream. Add the eggs and beat well. Pour into the pastry case smoothing down the surface with a wet palette knife. Bake for 30 minutes. Allow to cool completely in the tin before transferring to a serving plate. Decorate with icing sugar and a stencil and place a few liqueur-filled eggs on top, if liked.

[Puff

p a s t r y]

Puff pastry – the basis for layered galettes, flaky pastries, tarts, palmiers, cheese straws and mille-feuilles – is made by trapping fat within a soft flour-and-water paste. A series of turns and folds creates thin layers of fat and paste, one on top of the other, which form the flakes of the pastry as they cook.

Puff pastry is difficult to make: it requires a lot of care and a certain amount of dexterity when rolling. To make successful pastry, you need to follow the instructions given in the recipe to the letter so as to obtain regularly divided layers. Do not work in the heat. If you make puff pastry the day before, only finish the last two turns just before you use it.

Serves 6
(Makes a 26cm/10½in galette or tart)
200g/7oz strong white flour
100ml/3½fl oz water
1 tsp salt
About 150g/5oz butter or margarine (the weight of butter should equal that of the paste, the flour and water mixture)
2 or 3 tbsp caster sugar

The ingredients will produce 250g/9oz puff pastry.
For a larger or smaller amount, maintain the same proportions.

Preparation
Pour the flour into a mixing bowl and make a well in the centre. Salt the water and add to the well, mixing first with a wooden spoon then by hand. Knead quickly to form a dough. Make a ball and weigh it so as to calculate the right amount of fat to use. Leave the dough to rest for 15 to 20 minutes in a bowl covered with a clean, dry tea towel.

Lightly flour the work surface and roll out the dough to a rectangle about 30cm/12in x 20cm/8in that is slightly thicker in the middle. Ensure the fat is the same consistency as the paste (soften it a little with a spatula if necessary). Place on the lower half of the dough and fold the top of the dough over to enclose the butter in the middle. Press the edges together to form a seal. Roll this out into a rectangle 1cm/½in thick that is three times longer than it is wide. Apply

pressure evenly when rolling. The fat should not escape from the dough.

Fold the rectangle to form three layers, bringing the first third down over the middle towards you and the last third up over the top of the other two and away from you. Give the pastry a quarter turn so that the opening is on your right. This is called "giving a turn". Now give a second turn immediately: roll out into a rectangle again, fold into three, give a quarter turn to the right and chill for 20 minutes.

Classic puff pastry needs six turns – three lots of two turns, with a resting period in between each series of turns.

Cooking
Puff pastry should be place in the oven at a high temperature Gas 7/220°C/fan oven 200°C . The temperature will vary depending on the use.

Storing
Puff pastry can only be kept in the fridge for a few days, but it freezes well, both uncooked and cooked.

Apricot tricornes

Serves 4
PREPARATION TIME: 30 minutes
COOKING TIME: 15–20 minutes
plus resting time

400g/14oz puff pastry
6 ripe juicy apricots
12 blanched almonds
12 tbsp caster sugar
1 large pinch cinnamon
1 egg yolk
Icing sugar to decorate

Cut the puff pastry into four equal portions, using a knife. Roll out each portion on a lightly floured surface 4mm thick into a 15cm/6in circle. Use the tip of the rolling point to make three points, turning the circle into a triangular shape. Chill for 20 minutes.

Preheat oven to Gas 6/200°C/fan oven 180°C.

Wash and dry the apricots, slice in half and remove the stone. Place an almond in each of the apricot halves. Mix the sugar and cinnamon together. Take the pastry out of the fridge and place a tablespoon of the cinnamon sugar into the centre of each. Arrange three apricot halves on each one, with the rounded part uppermost. Cover each of the tricornes with two tablespoons of cinnamon sugar. Brush tricornes with egg yolk mixed with a little water. Place the pastries on a baking tray, evenly spaced apart. Fold the tip of each tricorne into the centre and pinch together to seal. Bake for 15–20 minutes until golden. Sprinkle with icing sugar and serve warm.

Apple and hazelnut turnovers ›

Makes 12 turnovers
PREPARATION TIME: 20 minutes
COOKING TIME: 20–25 minutes
plus resting time

3 apples
50g/2oz butter
50g/2oz caster sugar
½ tbsp vanilla sugar
50g/2oz shelled, blanched and
roughly chopped hazelnuts
500g/1lb 2oz puff pastry
1 egg yolk

Peel the apples, remove the cores and the pips, and slice. Pan-fry lightly in the butter for 5–10 minutes, or until softened. Mash lightly with a fork. Stir in the caster sugar, vanilla sugar and hazelnuts.

Preheat oven to Gas 6/200°C/fan oven 180°C. Roll out the pastry on a lightly floured surface until it is about 3mm/⅛in thick and cut into 12 circles with a 10cm/4in plain or fluted pastry cutter. Spoon the apple mixture onto one half of each of the circles, leaving a 2cm/¾in border around the edge. Moisten the edges with a little water, then fold the pastry over to cover the apples, crimping the edges together to seal.

Transfer the turnovers onto a baking sheet and leave to rest for 10 minutes. Brush the tops of the turnovers with the egg yolk mixed with a little water. Bake for 12–15 minutes until risen and golden. Serve warm or cold.

Puffed Almond Galette ▾

Serves 6 to 8
PREPARATION TIME: 20 minutes
COOKING TIME: 30 minutes

1 egg plus 1 yolk to glaze
100g/4oz caster sugar
100g/4oz ground almonds
25g/1oz melted butter
1 tbsp rum
800g/1lb 12oz puff pastry

Mix the egg, caster sugar and ground almonds together. Add the butter and flavour the mixture with the rum. Chill until ready to use.

Cut the pastry in half and roll out one half on a lightly floured surface. Cut out a 26cm/10½in circle. Roll out the remaining pastry and cut out a 28cm/11½in circle.

Preheat the oven to Gas 7/220°C/fan oven 200°C.

Lightly moisten a large baking sheet and place the smaller disk on top, taking care to keep its shape. Spread the almond paste in the middle, leaving a 2cm/¾in border at the edge. Brush the border with egg yolk. Place the larger circle on top and press the edges down well to seal. Flute the edges of the pastry, if liked, and score the top with the tip of a sharp knife. Brush the whole galette with the egg yolk. Chill for 30 minutes, then bake for 30 minutes.

Use a flexible knife to place the galette on a serving plate and serve warm.

COOK'S TIP
Traditionally, this cake is made for Epiphany (6 January). A bean is placed in the almond cream, bringing good luck to whoever finds it in their portion.

Spiced apple tart

Serves 6 to 8
PREPARATION TIME: 30 minutes
COOKING TIME: 20–25 minutes

330g/10½oz puff pastry
1 egg, separated
1kg/2lb 4oz firm tart apples
60g/2½oz lightly butter
75g/3oz brown sugar
½ tsp cinnamon
pinch grated nutmeg
2 turns of the pepper mill

Roll out the pastry on a lightly floured surface and use to line a 26cm/10½in pie tin . Brush the pastry base with the beaten egg white. Flute the edges of the pastry and brush with a little egg yolk.

Preheat the oven to Gas 9/240°C/fan oven 220°C. Peel and quarter the apples and remove the cores. If the apples are very large, halve each quarters.

Melt the butter in a large pan. As soon as it starts to turn pale, add the apples. Cook until they start to turn golden – this should take about 5 minutes – turn over and cook for a further 4-5 minutes. Don't allow them to become mushy. Remove from the heat and cool completely.

Mix the sugar, cinnamon, nutmeg and pepper. Arrange the apple pieces neatly on the pastry. Place in the oven for 15 minutes, then take out and sprinkle with the spiced sugar mixture. Return to the oven for another 10–15 minutes. Use a flat-bladed flexible knife to turn the tart out of the tin and onto a serving platter. Serve warm.

Savoy pear rézules

Makes 6
PREPARATION TIME: 30 minutes
COOKING TIME: 20–25 minutes

600g/1lb 5oz puff pastry
3 pears
150g/5oz caster sugar
Small piece of a stick
of cinnamon
Oil for frying
Icing sugar

Peel and quarter the pears and remove the cores. Place in a pan with the caster sugar and cinnamon. Cook on a low heat, stirring occasionally, until the pears have softened without turning into compote. Take off the heat, remove the cinnamon and cool.

Roll out the puff pastry on a lightly floured surface to about 3mm/⅛in thick. Using a pastry cutter or a small bowl, cut out six circles (as large as possible). Divide the pear mixture between them, placing onto the lower half of each circle and leaving at least a 1cm/½ border. Brush the edges with water and fold the upper part over the lower, aligning the edges and pressing down to seal.

Heat the oil in a large heavy-based pan until a piece of bread dropped in turns golden in 30 seconds. Put two of the pastries in at a time and fry until they rise to the surface. Use a slotted spoon to turn. When they are golden brown on both sides, remove and drain on kitchen paper. Keep warm while cooking the remaining pastries. Sprinkle generously with icing sugar and serve immediately.

Mille-feuilles

Makes 6
PREPARATION TIME: 1 hour,
plus resting time
COOKING TIME: 25 minutes

1 vanilla pod, split
500ml/18fl oz milk
4 egg yolks
100g/4oz caster sugar
40g/1½oz flour
40g/1½oz cornflour
25g/1oz butter
100ml/3½fl oz whipping cream
25–50ml/1–2fl oz golden rum
600g/1lb 5oz puff pastry
6 tbsp icing sugar

Scrape the seeds from the vanilla pod and place the pod and seeds into a large pan with the milk. Bring to the boil, then turn off the heat and leave to cool completely. Remove the vanilla pod and discard.

Beat the eggs and sugar together in a mixing bowl until the mixture turns a creamy white and thickens. Sift the flour and cornflour over and stir well to combine. Gradually stir in the infused milk. Pour the cream into a pan and cook over a low heat, stirring continuously until the mixture thickens. Stir in the butter. Pour into a bowl, cool, cover with cling film and place in the fridge.

Meanwhile, divide the puff pastry into three equal-size pieces. Roll out each piece on a lightly floured surface to a 30cm/12in square, then score each into six 30cm/12in x 10cm/4in to give you 18 segments. Prick with a fork and set aside to chill for 1 hour.

Preheat oven to Gas 7/220°C/fan oven 200°C. Moisten a baking sheet, put the three scored pastry squares on it and bake for 10 minutes on one side, then turn them over and cook for a further 5 minutes. Cool on a wire rack. Cut along the scored lined to give you 18 separate rectangles.

Beat the whipping cream until its forms soft peaks. Whisk the cold patisserie cream to add volume. Add the rum and gently fold in the whipped cream. Select six rectangles of pastry (the most solid) to make the bottom of the mille-feuille and lay side by side. Keep the six best ones for the top of the desssert. Spread a layer of patisserie cream over the base. Place the other rectangles not reserved for the top on top of these, ensuring that you line them up correctly. Spread with another layer of patisserie cream. Place the reserved rectangles carefully on top and press down lightly. Tidy the sides of the pastries using a spatula to smooth them. Dust generously with icing sugar and chill until ready to serve.

[Doughnut and beignet batter]

These batters are easy to make. There are a few basic rules to observe when you are making beignets, or fritters, and doughnuts:
- make the batter 1 or 2 hours before frying
- ensure the batter is not too runny
- the oil for frying needs to be kept at a steady temperature, without smoking (an electric deep-fat fryer maintains a constant temperature)
- drop the doughnuts quickly into the oil and fry in batches
- when making beignets from choux pastry which rises, the temperature of the oil should be lower at the beginning: start at 120°C/235°F and gradually increase to 175°C/335°F

For 18 to 20 beignets or doughnuts
125g/4½oz flour
1 large egg
½ tsp salt
1 tbsp caster sugar
1 tbsp oil
about 50ml/2fl oz milk, water or beer

Optional flavourings: lemon zest, a few drop of orange-flower water, 1 tbsp rum or other alcohol
Caster sugar or icing sugar to dust the doughnuts.

To make larger or smaller quantities, maintain the same proportions. Some recipes use slightly different ingredients for different doughnut and beignet batters. The proportions for the recipe are given in each case.

Preparation
Sift the flour into a bowl. Put the egg in the middle and add the salt and sugar. Pour in the oil and gently mix with a spatula or wooden spoon. Gradually add the milk (or half water and half milk for a lighter batter). Work the batter until it becomes smooth without being too liquid. Set aside for 1–2 hours.

Cooking (for ordinary beignets)
Heat the oil to 175°C/350°F. Drop a spoonful or ladleful of batter into the oil to form each beignet. Use a skimmer to turn the beignets after 1–2 minutes. When both sides are golden brown, lift out one by one and place on kitchen paper to drain. Dust with icing sugar or grated chocolate or serve with fruit coulis, if liked.

Storing
The batter keeps for up to 24 hours in the fridge.

Melon beignets

Serves 4
(makes about 12–14 beignets)
PREPARATION TIME: 30 minutes,
plus resting time
COOKING TIME: 25 minutes

1 ripe melon, with a good smell
and firm flesh
Flour
Flavourless oil for deep-frying
Caster sugar

ANISE CUSTARD
500ml/18fl oz milk
1 star anise
6 egg yolks
100g/4oz caster sugar

BEIGNET BATTER
120g/4½oz flour
1 medium egg + 3 egg whites
30g/1¼oz caster sugar
100ml/3½fl oz lager
1 tbsp anise-flavoured alcohol

Make the custard (see p. 81), substituting the star anise for the vanilla pod.

Make the batter (see p. 41), adding egg whites. Flavour with anise alcohol, mix and leave to rest for 1 hour.

Halve the melon, remove the seeds and cut the flesh into 12–16 thick slices. Remove the skins. Wipe each slice with kitchen paper and lightly flour so the batter will stick to the fruit.

Heat the oil in a large heavy-based pan or deep fryer until a piece of bread dropped in turns golden in 30 seconds. Dip the fruit into the batter, allowing any excess to drip away, then carefully lift into the hot oil (2–3 pieces of melon at a time) and fry for about 3 minutes until golden brown, turning them over halfway through cooking. Lift out and place on kitchen paper to drain. Coat each piece with caster sugar and keep warm while you cook the remaining melon beignets. Serve hot, with the anise-flavoured custard.

Chiquenaudes ›

Serves 8
PREPARATION TIME: 20 minutes
COOKING TIME: 20-30 minutes

400g/14oz flour
100g/4oz caster sugar
2 tbsp water
100g/4oz melted butter
4 eggs
1 tbsp orange-flower water
Oil for deep fat frying

COLOURED SUGAR
Granulated sugar
Red food colouring

Tip the flour onto a clean work surface and form a mound with a well. Put the caster sugar, water, butter and eggs in the middle. Add the orange-flower water. Work quickly and start to pull some of the flour into the liquid centre. Knead with the tips of the fingers, and then the hands, until small bubbles of air come to the surface of the dough.

Roll out the dough on a lightly floured surface to 3mm/⅛in thick. Use a knife or small cutters to cut geometric shapes (circles, squares and diamonds). You can also 'tear' it by hand, which is where the name of this dessert originally came from: French "déchiqueter" means tearing to pieces.

Heat the oil until a piece of bread dropped in turns golden in 30 seconds. Cook the shapes in batches for 2–3 minutes, until puffed slightly and golden brown. Drain on kitchen paper and keep warm while cooking the remaining shapes.

Make the coloured sugar: pour the granulated sugar into a covered container and add a few drops of red food colouring. Close and shake. Arrange the chiquenaudes on a plate and coat with the coloured sugar. Serve at once or leave to cool slightly.

Apple fritters ▾

Serves 6
(Makes 12 fritters)
PREPARATION TIME: 20 minutes,
plus resting time
COOKING TIME: 12-15 minutes

FOR THE FILLING
3 apples
1 tbsp caster sugar
2 tsp cognac, rum or orange-
flower water

FOR THE FRITTER BATTER
125g/4½oz flour
½ tsp salt
1 large egg
1 tbsp oil
1 tbsp caster sugar
Optional flavourings: lemon zest,
orange-flower water or alcohol
(rum, cognac...)
50ml/2fl oz water, milk or beer
Oil for deep-frying
50g/2oz caster sugar, to dredge

Make the filling: peel the apples, cut into slices and remove the cores. Put on a deep plate with the sugar and toss with your chosen flavouring.

Make the batter: sift the flour into a large bowl, make a well in the centre. Add the salt, sugar, egg, oil and flavouring into the middle. Mix from the centre with a wooden spoon, gradually adding more flour into the mixture. Add the liquid slowly and work the batter vigourously. It should be smooth and barely runny. Set aside for 2 hours.

Heat the oil until a piece of bread dropped in turns golden in 30 seconds. Cover a plate with kitchen paper. Check the batter – it should coat the back of a wooden spoon. Dip three or four apple rounds into the batter, making sure they are properly coated. Use two forks to remove them and dip them gently into the oil. Cook for 2–3 minutes, turning through cooking until golden brown and slightly puffed. Drain on the kitchen paper, sprinkle with sugar and serve immediately.

Madrid churros

Serves 4

(Makes about 16)

PREPARATION TIME: 10 minutes
COOKING TIME: 25–35 minutes

150g/5oz plain flour
250 ml/9fl oz water
½ tsp salt
Oil for deep-frying
Caster sugar

Sift the flour into a large mixing bowl and make a well in the centre.

Pour the water into a pan, add the salt and bring to the boil. Once boiling vigourously, pour the salted water quickly into the middle of the flour and beat with a wooden spoon until thick and glossy, leave to cool.

Put this paste into a large icing bag fitted with a 1cm/½in fluted nozzle.

Heat the oil in a large pan or deep fat fryer until a piece of bread dropped in turns golden in 60 seconds. Hold the icing bag over the deep fat fryer and squeeze out 15cm/6in long pieces, cutting them off from the piping nozzle with a wetted knife or scissors. Repeat to 4–5 times. Cook until golden brown, turning with a slotted spoon to ensure they are evenly cooked. Lift out, drain on kitchen paper and keep warm while cooking the remaining churros. Serve hot, dusted with caster sugar.

Berlin doughnuts

Serves 6

(Makes about 18 doughnuts)

PREPARATION TIME: 30 minutes,
plus resting time
COOKING TIME: 30 minutes

125ml/4fl oz milk
7g sachet fast-action dried yeast
400g/14oz strong flour
½ tsp salt
50g/2oz caster sugar
2 medium eggs, beaten
2 tsp lemon flavouring
Oil for deep-frying
Apricot jam (optional)
Icing sugar

Pour the milk into a pan, heat gently, until the milk is just hand-hot. Leave to cool slightly if necessary – if the milk is too hot it will kill the yeast. Sprinkle over the yeast and whisk until frothy and tiny air bubbles appear on the surface.

Sift the flour and salt into a large mixing bowl and make a well in the centre. Pour in the milk and stir in the caster sugar, eggs and lemon flavouring until it forms a smooth dough. Knead on a lightly floured surface for 6-8 minutes until smooth and elastic. Return to a clean lightly oiled bowl and cover with a clean cloth. Leave in a warm place for at least 3 hours until doubled in size. Remove from the bowl and knead for 2-3 minutes until smooth.

Divide the dough into 18 equal pieces, weighing about 50g/2oz each. Place well spaced on lightly oiled baking sheets. Cover again and leave to rise in a warm place for 30 minutes.

Heat the oil in a large pan or deep fat fryer until a piece of bread dropped in turns golden in 60 seconds. Cook the doughnuts in batches – they are cooked when they rise to the top and are golden brown and puffed. Drain on kitchen paper while cooking the rest. This dessert is traditionally served by cutting the doughnuts in half and filling with apricot jam.

Arrange on a plate in a pyramid and dust generously with icing sugar. Serve immediately.

[Choux

pastry]

Choux pastry – used for making éclairs, round custard-filled pastries, Paris-Brest and profiteroles – rises on account of the eggs and water that are beaten into the mixture. To make successful choux pastry, ensure that the flour is properly sifted and that the correct proportions of the ingredients are maintained.

Makes 18 average-sized choux balls
(1 tbsp pastry each)
150g/5oz flour
250ml/9fl oz water
75g/3oz butter
½ tsp salt
1 tbsp caster sugar
4 medium eggs

To make a larger or smaller amount, maintain the proportions given. Some recipes use slightly different ingredients to make choux pastry. The proportions for the recipe are given in each case.

Preparation

Sift the flour onto a sheet of grease-proof paper. Pour the water into a pan, cut the butter into small pieces and add together with the sugar and salt. Place on a high heat. Bring to the boil, remove from the heat and tip in all the flour at once, stirring quickly with a wooden spoon. The mixture should form a ball that comes away from the sides of the pan. If this doesn't happen, place the pan on a gentle heat and stir until the pastry is dry enough for this to happen.

Off the heat, break an egg and beat completely into the mixture before adding the other eggs, one by one. Check the consistency of the mixture: it should be firm and flexible. If it is too dry, add half of another egg. If still too dry, add the other half.

Lightly grease the baking tray. Using two teaspoons, scoop up the pastry, forming balls that are placed quite far apart on the tray (you can use a piping bag, held upright, instead of spoons and you may prefer to make éclairs by squeezing out regularly spaced sausage shapes). Start on the far side of the baking tray and work back towards yourself.

Cooking

This kind of pastry needs to be cooked at a high temperature Gas 7/220°C/ fan oven 200°C for 15–20 minutes. Place the baking tray in the middle of the oven. The choux balls are ready when they have risen to the surface and are golden brown in colour. Don't take them out until they are properly cooked or they will collapse.

Storing

Choux pastry can be kept in the fridge for 24 hours. It can also be frozen. If frozen, take out of the freezer around 12 hours before use.

Chocolate éclairs ›

Makes 6 to 8
PREPARATION TIME: 50 minutes
COOKING TIME: 20 minutes

CHOUX PASTRY
150g/5oz flour
250ml/9fl oz water
75g/3oz butter + some for the tin
Pinch salt
1 tbsp caster sugar
4 eggs

PATISSERIE CREAM
60g/2½oz plain chocolate
500ml/18fl oz milk
2 medium whole eggs + 1 yolk
60g/2½oz caster sugar
60g/2½oz plain flour

ICING
50g/2oz icing sugar
3 tbsp water
150g/5oz plain chocolate
30g/1¼oz butter

Make the choux pastry **(see p. 47)**. Preheat oven to Gas 6/ 200°C/fan oven 180°C. Lightly butter a baking tray. Fill an icing bag with a 1cm/½in plain nozzle with the pastry. Squeeze out regular strips or sausage shapes 10cm/4in long onto the tray, cutting the choux pastry at the end of the nozzle with a wet round-bladed knife. Place in the oven for 20 minutes until risen and golden brown, then leave to cool on a wire rack.

Make the patisserie cream: place the chocolate and milk into a small pan and cook over a low heat, stirring occasionally until the chocolate has melted. Beat the eggs, caster sugar and flour together in a mixing bowl until thick and smooth. Add this mixture to the chocolate milk and, stirring all the time, continue to cook over a low heat. As soon as the mixture starts to simmer, remove from the heat and leave to cool.

Use scissors to cut open the éclairs lengthways, along one side only, and fill with chocolate patisserie cream.

Make the icing: melt the icing sugar in less than a tablespoon of water; the mixture should be thick and barely liquid. Melt the chocolate in a bowl set over a pan of simmering water with two tablespoons of water and the butter. When it is all evenly mixed together, pour over the sugar and mix well. Ice each éclair by holding it vertically above the bowl and pouring a spoonful of icing so it runs down the éclair coating the top. Place on a rack to dry before serving.

Paris-Brest

Serves 6 to 8
PREPARATION TIME: 35 minutes
COOKING TIME: 45 minutes

CHOUX PASTRY
125g/4½oz flour
225ml/8fl oz water
60g/2½oz butter
Salt
1 tsp caster sugar
3 medium eggs

MERINGUE
4 egg whites
200g/7oz caster sugar

PRALINE CREAM
175g/6oz butter
3 egg yolks
200g/7oz praline, crushed

DECORATION
25g/1oz icing sugar

Preheat the oven to Gas 6/ 200°C/fan oven 180°C.

Make the choux pastry **(see p. 47)**. Fill an icing bag with a 2cm/¾in fluted nozzle with the pastry. Lightly greased a baking sheet and pipe a 22cm/8¾in circle. Bake for 45 minutes in the oven until this ring is pale golden, dry and light. Take out of the oven and place on a wire rack to cool before slicing in half lengthways.

Make the meringue: place a large bowl over a pan of barely simmering water. Add the egg whites and caster sugar and whisk with an electric whisk for 8–10 minutes until they form a shiny white firm meringue mixture. Cool.

Make the praline cream: soften the butter with a spatula or wooden spoon. Add the egg yolks and praline. Beat thoroughly and then gently incorporate the cold meringue mixture. Chill.

Fill the choux pastry ring with the meringue mixture, using an icing bag with a 1.5cm/5/8in fluted nozzle. Place the lid on top and dust with icing sugar before serving.

Gateau Saint Honoré

Serves 8 to 10
PREPARATION TIME: 1 hour 30 minutes plus resting time
COOKING TIME: 1 hour 10 minutes

SHORTCRUST PASTRY (FOR THE BASE)
150g/5oz flour
75g/3oz butter
1 egg yolk
250ml/9fl oz water
½ tsp salt

CHOUX PASTRY
125g/4½oz flour
225ml/8fl oz water
60g/2½oz butter
½ tsp salt
1 sugar lump
3 eggs

CARAMEL
150g/5oz sugar lumps
½ tsp vinegar

SAINT-HONORÉ CREAM
2 leaves gelatine
250ml/9fl oz milk
1 vanilla pod
3 egg yolks
1 tbsp rum (optional)
100g/4oz caster sugar
20g/¾oz flour
5 egg whites

Make the shortcrust pastry for the base **(see p. 21)**. Leave to rest for 20 minutes while making the choux pastry.

Preheat the oven to Gas 6/200°C/fan oven 180°C.

Roll out the shortcrust pastry to 5mm/¼in thick and place carefully on a barely greased baking tray. Carefully cut out a 25cm/10in circle and remove the remaining pastry scraps. Prick with a fork to prevent the pastry rising during cooking.

Fill a piping bag with a 1.2cm/½in plain nozzle full of choux pastry. Pipe a ring of choux pastry right around the edge of the base and continue round, forming a spiral leading into the centre. Pipe the remaining choux mixture into about twenty small walnut-sized balls. Bake for 25–30 minutes then remove the choux balls only and continue to bake the base for a further 15 minutes. The pastry should be a pale golden colour.

Make a pale golden caramel of sugar lumps moistened with water in a pan with tapered sides (see p. 16). Add a little vinegar to prevent the caramel hardening too quickly. Very carefully coat each of the balls by dipping the top into the caramel. Stick them onto the outside ring of the choux base, touching one another, ensuring the caramel sides face upwards.

Make the Saint-Honoré cream: soften the gelatine leaves in a bowl of cold water for 15 minutes. Split the vanilla pod in two, scrape out the seeds and add the seeds and pod to the milk. Heat and leave to infuse. Discard the pod. Mix the egg yolks, caster sugar and flour together until well combined. Add the hot vanilla-flavoured milk. Stirring continuously, cook on a low heat until it begins to simmer. Remove from the heat and add the gelatine. Flavour with rum if desired.

Whisk the egg whites until stiff. Continue beating with a hand-whisk while pouring the hot cream onto the egg whites to form a light cream. Cool. Fill the hollow centre of the choux ring with the mixture, using two spoons: as it cools, the gelatine will make it set, and if the cream has been made properly, the marks made by the spoons will remain visible, like crests on the surface.

VARIATION: To simplify making this dessert, you can use whipped cream instead of Saint-Honoré cream **(see p. 95)**.

Cherry profiteroles ▸

Serves 6
PREPARATION TIME: 30–40 minutes
COOKING TIME: 20 minutes

500ml/18fl oz vanilla ice cream
150g/5oz cherries in brandy
200g/7oz fresh cherries
30g/1¼oz caster sugar
½ tbsp vanilla sugar
50ml/2fl oz kirsch
12 large choux balls

Take the vanilla ice cream out of the freezer and leave at room temperature until it softens, without letting it melt. Stone the brandied cherries and add to the ice cream, combining as quickly as possible. Replace in the freezer.

Meanwhile, wash, tail and stone the fresh cherries. Put in a pan with the caster sugar and vanilla sugar. Cook for 20 minutes on a low heat, stirring occasionally to reduce to compote. Half-cover with a lid as necessary. When the cherries are cooked, heat the kirsch, set it alight and pour onto the cherries. Scrape the bottom well with a wooden spoon to deglaze the juices.

Just before serving, cut open the choux and fill with a ball of the brandied cherry ice cream. Place two profiteroles on each plate accompanied by the compote. Serve immediately.

Easter egg croquembouche

Serves 10 to 12
PREPARATION TIME: 2 hours
COOKING TIME: 20 minutes

PATISSERIE CREAM
75ml/2½fl oz milk
1 vanilla pod
2 eggs + 2 yolks
100g/4oz caster sugar
100g/4oz plain flour
30g/1¼oz butter, cut
into small pieces
2 tbsp rum or orange liqueur
60 choux balls

CARAMEL
80 sugar lumps
12 tbsp water

Make a patisserie cream: heat the milk with the split, scraped vanilla pod and seeds. Beat the whole eggs, yolks and caster sugar together in a bowl until the mixture becomes thick and creamy. Sift in the flour and combine. Strain and gradually add the hot infused milk to the egg mixture. Pour this cream into the rinsed pan and continue to stir with a wooden spoon while cooking over a gentle heat until it thickens (about 5 minutes). Remove from the heat. Add the butter and the alcohol of your choice to flavour your dessert. Cool – the cream should be fairly thick.

Open a hole in the bottom of the choux balls and fill with the cream using a piping bag with a narrow nozzle.

Make the caramel for sticking the choux balls together to form the egg: put 20 sugar lumps moistened with water into a pan and heat gently until the sugar has dissolved and forms a pale golden caramel (see p. 16). Use the remaining sugar lumps to make as much caramel as required, in about three portions.

To assemble the egg, stick four choux balls together on a flat plate, keeping a clear border around them. To do this, hold each choux ball by the bottom and dip quickly into the caramel. Repeat using five balls to form a slightly larger circular layer on top. Repeat, using nine balls, then twelve. The egg is now at the halfway stage. Use the remaining 30 balls to form decreasing circular layers (of twelve, nine, five and four balls respectively) so as to form a large egg.

Keep the egg in a cool place (not in the fridge) until serving. Decorate with a ribbon and serve.

[Crêpes, pancake and waffle batter]

Make the batter 1 or 2 hours before cooking crêpes (thin pancakes) or waffles. For speedy crêpes select two very shallow heavy-bottomed crêpe pans and do not pour in too much batter in one go.
Some recipes use slightly different ingredients for different batters. The proportions for the recipe are given in each case.

Crêpe batter

Makes 12 average crêpes
250g/9oz flour
500ml/18fl oz milk (or half milk/half water)
3 medium eggs
2 tbsp melted butter or oil
½ tsp fine salt
2 tbsp caster sugar
Optional flavourings: lemon zest, 1 tsp vanilla sugar, 1 tbsp rum or liqueur
Butter or oil for cooking

Preparation
Tip the flour into a large bowl and make a well in the centre. Pour in half of the milk. Beginning in the centre, draw the flour gradually into the milk, mixing in with a wooden spoon.

Whisk the eggs briefly, then stir into the mixture. Add the butter or oil, salt and caster sugar. Continue stirring and gradually add the rest of the milk – the batter should flow readily but not be too runny. Add your chosen flavouring. Cover the bowl with a clean cloth and set aside for 1 to 2 hours at room temperature. If the batter is too thick, add a little water.

This batter is easily made by mixing all the ingredients in a food processor. Make sure the bowl does not overflow!

Cooking
Pour half a ladle of batter (about 2 tablespoons) into a hot, greased pan. Tip the pan up so that the batter coats it evenly. After a few second the edges of the crêpe start to curl up. Use a flexible spatula to turn it over and cook the other side. Slide the crêpe on to warm plate on top of a pan of boiling water. Season according to taste.

Waffle batter

Makes about 12 waffles
500ml/18fl oz milk
100g/4oz butter
250g/9oz flour
150g/5oz caster sugar
3 eggs
1 pinch salt
1 tsp baking powder
Optional flavourings: lemon zest, 1 tbsp orange-flower water or rum, or 1 tsp vanilla sugar
Butter or oil for cooking

Preparation
Warm the milk and melt the butter in it. Put the flour into a mixing bowl and make a well in the centre. Add the caster sugar, eggs and salt. Using a wooden spoon, slowly draw the flour in and the baking powder. Add the milk gradually so that the mixture does not become too thick. The batter should be thoroughly beaten and without lumps. Add the chosen flavouring.

Cooking
Heat a waffle iron and brush the plates with butter or oil. Quickly pour two or three tablespoons of batter in to fill up to the mould level covering all the moulds in the waffle iron. Close the waffle iron. Each waffle takes from 2 to 5 minutes to cook. When the waffle is cooked, remove from the iron and place on a cooling rack for a few seconds. Waffles quickly become hard and crunchy. Season according to taste and repeat until there is no batter mixture left.

Crêpe and waffle batter can be kept in the fridge for 24 hours.

Flambé crêpes with citrus butter

Serves 4
(Makes 12 crêpes)
PREPARATION TIME: 5 minutes
COOKING TIME: 15 minutes

100g/4oz butter
1 unwaxed orange
1 unwaxed lemon
1 unwaxed lime
2 tbsp icing sugar
12 crêpes
50ml/2fl oz rum
50ml/2fl oz orange liqueur

Take the butter out of the fridge and leave to soften at room temperature. Brush the citrus fruit under hot water to wash. Grate half the peel to make zest, squeeze out the juice and set aside.

Cream the butter, icing sugar and citrus zests until smooth and well combined. Divide the butter into two equal pieces and add one piece each to two 23cm/9in frying pans. Melt over a low heat. Fold the crêpes in half three times to form eighths and put six of them in each pan, heating them for two minutes on either side.

Combine the rum and orange liqueur and pour onto the crêpes. Set alight. As soon as the flames go out, remove the crêpes from the pan and arrange them in a rosette on a plate. Deglaze the sauce in the pans with the citrus juice, stirring on a high heat to get a syrupy consistency. Pour onto the crêpes and serve immediately.

Vanilla crêpes ›

Serves 8
(Makes 24 crêpes)
PREPARATION TIME: 30 minutes,
plus resting time
COOKING TIME: 30 minutes

500ml/18fl oz milk
100g/4oz butter
2 vanilla pods
250g/9oz flour
½ tsp salt
2 tbsp caster sugar +
extra to sprinkle over the crêpes
3 eggs

Pour the milk into a pan and add the butter. Split the vanilla pods in two lengthways and scrape out the small seeds inside. Put everything in the pan and bring to the boil. Take off the heat and leave to infuse for 15 minutes, then discard the vanilla pods.

Mix the flour, salt and caster sugar together in a large bowl and make a well in the centre. Break in the eggs. Adding the milk in a thin stream, gradually beat the mixture until it forms a smooth, runny batter – add a few spoonfuls of water if the mixture is too thick. Set aside to rest for 1 hour.

Cook the crêpes **(see p. 55)**. As soon as a crêpe is ready, place it on a plate and sprinkle with sugar before covering it with the next crêpe . Repeat until all the batter is finished. Serve warm or cold.

Pear soufflé crêpes

Serves 4
(Makes 12 crêpes)
PREPARATION TIME: 45 minutes,
plus resting time
COOKING TIME: 12 minutes

CRÊPE BATTER
150g/5oz flour
250ml/9fl oz milk
2 large eggs
1 tbsp caster sugar
Pinch salt
2 tbsp oil

FILLING
3 egg whites
150g/5oz caster sugar
2 large soft pears (comice)
2 tbsp water
3 sponge fingers
3 tbsp pear brandy or eau-de-vie
50g/2oz icing sugar

Make the crêpe batter **(see p. 55)** and set aside for 1 hour to rest (if it is too thick, add a few tablespoons of water).

Cook a dozen thin crêpes.

Make the filling: beat the egg whites and caster sugar in a mixing bowl over a bain-marie, using an electric whisk, until the mixture forms a shiny firm meringue. Peel and slice the pears and remove the centres. Stew with the water to make compote. Allow to cool. Mix with the meringue. Cut the sponge fingers into small pieces, moisten with the pear brandy or eau-de-vie and carefully fold them into the soufflé mixture.

Preheat oven to Gas 7/220°C/fan oven 200°C. Put a tablespoon of the mixture in the middle of each crêpe. Roll the edges in to form slightly open square packets. Place the crêpe packets side by side on an ovenproof serving dish. Sift icing sugar over the top and place in the oven for 12 minutes. Serve immediately.

‹ Lemon crêpe gateau

Serves 4
PREPARATION TIME: 20 minutes,
plus resting time
COOKING TIME: 50 minutes

CRÊPE BATTER
150g/5oz flour
300ml/½ pint milk
2 large eggs
2 tbsp oil
1 pinch salt
2 tbsp sugar
Lemon zest
A little butter for pan and tin

LEMON CURD
3 eggs
200g/7oz caster sugar
3 lemons
75g/3oz butter

DECORATION
Icing sugar

Make the crêpe batter **(see p. 55)** and set aside for 1 hour (if it is too thick, add a couple of tablespoons of water). Pour a small ladle of batter into a buttered crêpe pan and cook until the crêpe has dried. Repeat until there is no more batter left.

Make the lemon curd: mix the eggs, caster sugar, grated zest and juice of the lemons together in a stainless steel pan and cook on a low heat until creamy and thickened slightly. Pass the mixture through a fine sieve to remove the peel. Cut the butter into small pieces, add whisk into the lemon mixture. Allow to cool – the mixture should thicken again slightly on cooling.

Preheat oven to Gas 6/ 200°C/fan oven 180°C. Butter a deep sandwich tin of the same size as the crêpes. Put a crêpe on the bottom and cover with a fine layer of the lemon curd. Place a second crêpe on top, followed by another layer of curd. Repeat until there are no ingredients left, finishing with a crêpe on top. Bake for 20 minutes. After cooking, leave to cool before taking out of the tin. Sift with icing sugar before serving.

Orange-flower waffles ›

Serves 8
(Makes about 24 waffles)
PREPARATION TIME: 20 minutes
COOKING TIME: 1 hour

4 medium eggs
250g/9oz caster sugar
330g/10½oz flour
500ml/18fl oz milk
50ml/12fl oz water
Pinch salt
1 tbsp vanilla sugar
125g/4½oz melted butter + some
for the waffle iron (optional)
2 tbsp orange-flower water
Icing sugar

Separate the eggs. Beat the yolks and caster sugar together until pale and thick. Add the flour and dilute with the milk and water. Whip the egg whites with the salt and vanilla sugar until stiff. Add to the batter mixture. Finally add the butter and orange-flower water.

Heat the waffle iron (if it is not non-stick then grease it with butter for each waffle). Use a small ladle to pour the batter into the waffle iron until it reaches the cavities, but no higher (to avoid overflowing). Cook each waffle for about 3 minutes on one side and about 2 minutes on the other. Remove and keep warm while cooking the remaining waffles. Dust generously with icing sugar and serve.

Dry waffles with brown sugar

Serves 10
(Makes about 30 waffles)
PREPARATION TIME: 20 minutes,
plus overnight resting
COOKING TIME: 30 minutes

125ml/4fl oz milk
330g/10½oz butter
150g/5oz demerara sugar
200g/7oz flour
1 egg + 1 yolk

Cut the butter into small pieces and place in a pan on a low heat with the milk and brown sugar, stirring continuously until melted. In a mixing bowl, whisk the flour, egg and yolk, together with the milk, butter and sugar to form a smooth batter. Cover with a clean cloth and leave to rest for 12 hours.

Use a flat waffle pan. Unless it is non-stick, butter it every time you use it. Cook the first waffle: pour a spoonful into the waffle pan. As soon as it is ready, lift out of the pan and roll immediately to form a cornet. Don't wait until the waffle cools as it will become dry and break easily, and you won't be able to roll it. Repeat until there is no batter left.

These waffles can be served with cream, ice cream, mousse or fruit salad. They keep well stored in an airtight container.

[Mixtures that rise and their variations]

Yeast dough

Made with bakers' or brewers' yeast, this dough is used for babas, savarins, brioches, sugar tarts and gugelhupf. Versatile and easy to make, it holds its shape well and can be enriched with raisins and candied fruit. If you are making a savarin, you can use whipped cream, patisserie cream, compote or fruit salad to fill the middle.

Serves 6

150g/5oz flour
½ tsp salt
1 tbsp caster sugar
2 medium eggs
50ml/2fl oz milk
15g/½oz yeast
70g/2¾oz melted butter + and some for greasing the tin

Preparation

Put the flour into a mixing bowl and make a well in the centre. Add the salt, caster sugar and lightly beaten eggs. Crumble the yeast into the warm milk and add to the mixture, mixing well with a wooden spoon. Add the butter and work together to form a soft, smooth dough.
Cover the mixing bowl with a cloth and place in a warm place away from drafts for about 2 hours (the rising time will depend on the ambient temperature). The dough is ready when it has doubled in size.
Butter the tin well. Divide the dough and knead lightly by hand, without beating (the dough will collapse). Place the dough in the tin, ensuring that it only occupies the bottom third

and never more. Leave to rest for a bit longer: the dough will rise again to within 1cm/½in of the edge of the tin.

Cooking

Preheat oven to Gas 7/220°C/fan oven 200°C and place in the oven for 25 to 30 minutes. Check the dough is cooked before removing from the oven: it should be pale golden brown.

Baking powder mixtures

These mixtures are used to make fruit cakes, pound cakes, biscuits and shaped gateaux.
Baking powder is the last ingredient to be added as it reacts with moisture and produces carbon dioxide that can rapidly evaporate. When it is added too early in the recipe, it doesn't work properly and the cakes don't rise, as they should. There is no basic recipe for baking powder mixtures as the ingredients and proportions vary from one recipe to the next.

Egg white sponge mixtures

The lightness and volume of this mixture is created by stiffly beaten egg whites, which are carefully incorporated into the other ingredients. Heat makes it increase in size.
It is used for making sponge fingers and soufflés.
There is no basic recipe for making this kind of mixture as its ingredients vary according to the recipe.
There are several basic rules to remember:
- Take care when separating yolks and whites. There should be no trace of

yolk in the white or it will not beat properly
- Eggs stored in the fridge should be taken out an hour before they are needed
- You can't beat fresh eggs, laid on the same day
- When you find it difficult to get the egg whites to stiffen, add a pinch each of salt and caster sugar
- In order to ensure the beaten egg whites form a single lump, hold the bowl under cold water and do not wipe before starting
- For best results, beat egg whites in a deep bowl with a rounded base
- Always wait until the last minute to beat egg white until stiff (they don't stay stiff for long).

When adding beaten egg whites to a mixture

- Keep away from heat and avoid rapid movements.
- Incorporate whites by delicately lifting and slicing into the mixture with a spatula in a figure-of-eight. This is called "folding in". Do not turn the spatula over as this breaks up air bubbles and the mixture loses it lightness.
- Begin by gently adding a tablespoon of whisked whites into the mix, and then add the rest in one go, lifting the mixture to coat the whites. Fold gently.

Cooking

The tin should be placed on a low shelf in a moderate oven. Avoid opening the oven until the cake has risen properly, so that it doesn't collapse.

Fruit cake ▸

Serves 8
PREPARATION TIME: 25 minutes
COOKING TIME: 50 minutes

100g/4oz raisins
100g/4oz currants
200ml/7floz rum
150g/5oz candied fruit
175g/3oz butter+ some to grease
the tin
125g/4½oz caster sugar
Pinch salt
3 large eggs
250g/9oz flour
1 tsp baking powder

The day before making the cake, wash and dry the raisins. Leave to macerate in the rum with the finely chopped candied fruit.

The following day cut the butter into small pieces and leave to soften at room temperature. Preheat oven to Gas 7/220°C/fan oven 200°C. Cream the butter using a wooden spoon or electric whisk. Add the caster sugar, a little at a time, beating well, then add the salt and continue beating: the mixture should be pale and creamy. Add the eggs, one at a time, and beat well. Add the baking powder to the flour. Siift into the butter mixture. Incorporate to form a smooth mixture. Finally, add the macerated fruits and any remaining rum from the maceration. Mix until smooth.

Grease a 24cm/9½in long rectangular cake tin and line with greased baking paper. Spoon the mixture into the tin.

Place the cake in the oven for 10 minutes, then reduce the temperature to Gas 4/180°C/fan oven 160°C. After 30 minutes, reduce the temperature again to Gas 3/160°C/fan oven 140°C. Cook for a further 10 minutes until the cake has risen and is golden brown. Take out of the oven, lift it out of the tin and cool on a wire rack.

COOK'S TIP: To stop fruits dropping to the bottom, maintain the correct proportions of flour and sugar. Add mixture to the tin one spoon at a time.

Rum baba

Serves 6
PREPARATION TIME: 20 minutes,
plus resting + rising time
COOKING TIME: 30 minutes

YEAST DOUGH
150g/5oz flour
½ tsp salt
1 tbsp caster sugar
2 medium eggs
about 50ml/2fl oz milk
15g/½oz yeast
70g/2¾oz melted butter +
some for the tin

SYRUP
500ml/18fl oz water or tea
250g/9oz caster sugar
½ tbsp vanilla sugar
6 tbsp rum

FILLING (OPTIONAL)
Fruits (fresh or preserved) or
whipped cream

Make a yeast dough **(see p. 63)** and preheat oven to Gas 7 220°C/fan oven 200°C. Butter a savarin tin (a cylindrical baba tin) and fill with up to a third of the height with dough. Leave to rest until the dough has risen to 1cm/½in of the rim. Place in the oven for 30 minutes.

Meanwhile prepare the syrup: pour the water or tea, caster sugar and vanilla sugar into a stainless steel pan. Bring to the boil, remove from the heat and add the rum.

Take the baba out of the oven when it is cooked. Remove from the tin and place on a serving dish. Pour the hot syrup over it and leave to absorb for a minimum of 2 hours. Serve the baba as it is or garnish with preserved fruits or whipped.

‹ Gugelhupf

Serves 6 to 8

PREPARATION TIME: 40 minutes,
plus resting time
COOKING TIME: 45 minutes

250ml/9fl oz milk
20g fresh yeast
150g/5oz butter+ 25g/1oz
for the tin
1 pinch salt
100g/4oz caster sugar
500g/1lb 2oz flour
2 large eggs
125g/4½oz raisins
50g/2oz whole unblanched
almonds
Icing sugar

Warm the milk (hand hot - 30°C/86°F). Put four or five spoonfuls into a bowl. Crumble the yeast into the bowl. Stir and leave to rest. Melt the remaining butter with the salt and caster sugar in the remaining milk.

Sift the flour into a warmed mixing bowl, form a well and break the eggs into the centre. Stirring with a wooden spoon, gradually add the buttery milk and then the baking powder.

Work this elastic dough by lifting and kneading it but don't beat it. It is ready when it no longer sticks to your hands. Add the raisins. Cover with a clean cloth. Leave to rise in a warm place for 1½–2 hours, until it doubles in volume, then divide and gently knead again.

Generously butter a Gugelhupf tin and put a whole almond in each of the divisions in the bottom of the tin. Place the dough gently on top so the almonds are not displaced. Cover the tin and leave in a warm place until the dough has risen to fill it. Preheat oven to Gas 7/220°C/fan oven 200°C.

Place in the middle of the oven for 30 minutes. If the surface browns too quickly, cover with baking paper. Continue cooking for a further 15 minutes and check that the cake is ready by pricking it with a metal skewer: it should come out dry. Remove the gugelhupf, take it out of the tin and cool. It is best served the following day, after being sprinkled with icing sugar.

Lemon soufflé

Serves 4

PREPARATION TIME: 20 minutes
COOKING TIME: 30–40 minutes

1 unwaxed lemon
1 unwaxed lime
250ml/9fl oz milk
150g/5oz caster sugar
4 eggs + 1 egg white
3 tbsp cornflour
20g/¾oz butter+
some for the tin

Preheat oven to Gas 6/200°C/fan oven 180°C. Scrub the lemon and lime, finely grate the peel and squeeze the juice. Set a few slivers of zest aside to decorate.

Put the milk and caster sugar in a pan and bring to a simmer. Remove from the heat and put the zest in to infuse until needed.

Break the eggs and separate the whites and yolks. Set aside.

Put the cornflour in a bowl with 4 tablespoons of the filtered citrus juice. Add the mixture to the milk pan and place on a gentle heat to thicken.

Take off the heat and add the butter and yolks. Mix well and leave to cool completely.

Beat the egg white until stiff and delicately incorporate in the cold lemon mixture.

Butter a large soufflé mould and fill to two-thirds full with the mixture.

Place in the middle of the oven and cook for 30–40 minutes, until the soufflé has risen. Decorate with the citrus zest and serve immediately.

Orange fondant cake

Serves 6
PREPARATION TIME: 20 minutes
COOKING TIME: 30 minutes

CAKE MIXTURE
100g/4oz butter
100g/4oz caster sugar
2 eggs
100g/4oz flour
1 large orange
1 tsp baking powder

ICING
150g/5oz icing sugar
1 large juicy orange

Preheat oven to Gas 6/200°C/fan oven 180°C.

Cream the butter with a wooden spoon in a warm mixing bowl. Gradually beat in the caster sugar and add the eggs, one by one, continuing to beat. Add the flour, the finely grated zest and juice of the orange, keeping a few thin slivers of zest aside for decoration. Finally, add the baking powder. Butter a deep 24cm/9½in sandwich tin, preferably square, and pour in the mixture. Place in the oven for 30 minutes.

Make the icing: dissolve the icing sugar in the orange juice (you don't need to use all of the juice) making a thick runny cream.

When the gateau has finished cooking, remove from the tin. Put on a serving plate and pour half over the icing over while it is still hot. The cake will become soft. When it is cold, spread the remaining icing over and decorate with the slivers of orange zest.

Doughnuts

**Serves 6
(Makes 18 doughnuts)**
PREPARATION TIME: 40–45 minutes,
plus resting time
COOKING TIME: 20–25 minutes

250ml/9fl oz milk
20g fresh yeast
1 tsp salt
500g/1lb 2oz flour
60g/2½oz butter
150g/5oz brown sugar
2 eggs
Grated nutmeg
Oil for deep-frying
Icing sugar
Jam (optional)

Warm the milk, pour into a mixing bowl and crumble the yeast into it. Add the salt, 330g/10½oz of flour and beat thoroughly to make a smooth creamy mixture. Cover with a cloth and leave to rise for 30 minutes to 1 hour.

When it has risen, melt the butter and add to the mixture with the brown sugar, lightly beaten eggs, a little grated nutmeg and the remaining flour. Beat thoroughly and then knead. Leave to rise for 2–3 hours.

Knead again by hand. If the dough is too sticky, add a little more flour.

Cut the dough into 18 equal pieces using kitchen scissors. Roll to form thin 15cm/6in sausages. Join the ends of each together to form rings that measure roughly 9cm/3½in across.

Heat the oil for deep-frying: it should be boiling hot but not smoking. Fry the doughnuts three at a time: they should sink to the bottom and rise up again at once.

Cook for about 2 minutes until they start to turn golden brown, then turn over with a skimmer and cook for 1–2 minutes on the other side.

Place the doughnuts on a wire rack covered in kitchen paper to drain.

Arrange on a plate and coat liberally with icing sugar. You can fill them with jam by slicing in half through the middle. Serve hot, warm or cold.

Pound cake ▲

Serves 6 to 8
PREPARATION TIME: 20 minutes
COOKING TIME: 30–40 minutes

3 large eggs
200g/7oz butter + some
for the tin
200g/7oz caster sugar
200g/7oz plain flour

Cream the butter using a spatula, wooden spoon (fork or electric beater). Add a third of the caster sugar and beat thoroughly. Repeat for the rest of the sugar and beat until creamy.

Separate the egg whites and yolks. Add the yolks to the mixture. Sift and add the flour.

Preheat oven to Gas 5/190°C/fan oven 170°C.

Beat the egg whites until stiff and gently fold into the mixture, lifting carefully to maintain the lightness of the whites. The mixture should be soft but firm.

Butter a rectangular cake tin and fill with the mixture. Place in the middle of the oven for 30 minutes. Check that the cake is cooked by inserting the tip of a knife (it should come out dry). Continue cooking for another 10 minutes if necessary.

Remove from the oven and wait for 5 minutes before turning the cake out of the tin and onto a wire rack to cool. Serve cold.

Gateau de ménage

Serves 6

PREPARATION TIME: 30 minutes, plus resting time
COOKING TIME: 10 -15 minutes

400ml/14fl oz milk
40g/1½oz yeast
100g/4oz butter
100g/4oz margarine
1kg/2lb 4oz flour
Salt
200g/7oz caster sugar
4 eggs + 3 yolks
4 tbsp orange-flower water
500ml/18fl oz crème fraîche
Icing sugar to dust

Warm the milk and add 2 tablespoons to the baking powder. Pour the rest of the warm milk into a large mixing bowl with the butter and margarine that should melt. Cover with a cloth and set aside.

Pile the flour in a mixing bowl and form a well. Add 8 tablespoons of caster sugar, a little salt and the lightly beaten whole eggs. Beat until smooth. Add the butter and margarine mixture, the dissolved baking powder and 2 tablespoons of orange-flower water. Work the dough with a wooden spoon or spatula, then knead by hand to incorporate air. Cover with a cloth and set aside to rest in a warm place for 2–2½ hours. It is ready when the dough has tripled in volume.

Knead again and divide into six pieces.

Roll out each piece of dough and place in small round individual 10cm/4in tart tins, pinching the edges. Set aside to rise again.

Beat the crème fraîche, three egg yolks, six tablespoons of caster sugar and two of orange-flower water together in a bowl. Preheat oven to Gas 7/220°C/fan oven 200°C.

When the dough has risen in the cases, gently flatten the centre (as for a tart). Divide the egg yolk mixture between the tins and cook in the oven for 10–15 minutes. Take out of the oven and dust with icing sugar. Serve the dessert warm or cold.

Carrot cake ›

Serves 6

PREPARATION TIME: 20 minutes
COOKING TIME: 45 minutes

250g/9oz flour
1 tsp baking powder
1 tsp ground cinnamon
½ tsp salt
100g/4oz grated carrots
80g/3¼oz to
125g/4½oz raisins
50g/2oz chopped walnuts
100g/4oz demerara sugar
2 eggs
225ml/8fl oz milk
150g/5oz melted butter

Preheat oven to Gas 4/180°C/fan oven 160°C.

Mix the flour, baking powder, cinnamon and salt together in a bowl. Mix the grated carrots, raisins and walnuts together in another bowl. Add the demerara sugar, the lightly beaten eggs, milk and melted butter.

Combine the two mixtures and put into a rectangular cake tin lined with baking paper (bottom and sides). Bake for 45 minutes. Remove and leave to cool before taking out of the tin. Serve the gateau. cut into slices and arranged on a serving plate.

Pamplona gateau

Serves 10
PREPARATION TIME: 35 minutes
COOKING TIME: 30 minutes

CAKE MIXTURE
250g/9oz flour
250g/9oz caster sugar
4 tbsp cocoa powder
1 tsp ground cinnamon
1 tsp baking powder
100ml/3½fl oz milk
100ml/3½fl oz peanut oil
225ml/8fl oz water
125g/4½oz butter+
some for the tin
1 tsp vanilla extract
2 eggs

ICING
175g/6oz rich dark chocolate
2 tbsp water
125ml/4fl oz crème fraîche

DECORATION
1 tbsp cocoa powder

Make the cake mixture: mix the flour, caster sugar, cocoa powder, cinnamon and baking powder together. Form a well. Warm the milk, oil and water together in a pan. Add the butter as soon as it melts, remove from the heat and add the vanilla. Stir to make a smooth mixture and pour into the bowl, stirring continuously.

Preheat oven to Gas 5/190°C/fan oven 170°C.

Lightly beat the eggs and add to the bowl. Mix together. Butter a 40cm/16in square cake tin (or two smaller tins) and fill with the mixture. Place in the oven for 30 minutes. Take the gateau out of the oven and turn onto a wire rack to cool.

Make the icing: break the chocolate into squares and melt over a bain-marie with the water. When it softens, stir with a wooden spoon, add the crème fraîche and beat. Let the icing cool. When it has thickened enough but has not become too solid, cover the gateau.

Serve cold, not chilled, lightly dusted with cocoa powder.

Yoghurt and raisin gateau

Serves 8
PREPARATION TIME: 30 minutes
COOKING TIME: 45 minutes

330g/10½oz flour
180g/6¼oz caster sugar
1 pinch salt
2 tsp baking powder
4 eggs
250g/9oz natural yoghurt
1 tsp oil
20g butter for greasing the tin
250g/9oz raisins
250g/9oz currants

Preheat oven to Gas 6/ 200°C/fan oven 180°C.

Mix the flour, caster sugar, salt and baking powder together in a large mixing bowl and make a well in the centre. Break the eggs into another bowl and beat with the yoghurt. Tip the mixture into the well and beat with an electric mixer, adding the oil. Butter a deep 25cm/10in sandwich tin, and fill with the mixture.

Remove any stems from the raisins and currants and wash carefully. Dry with kitchen paper and then push them into the mix, alternating them.

Place in the middle of the oven pendant 45 minutes. Check that the gateau is cooked by inserting the point of a knife: it should come out clean and dry. If it doesn't, continue cooking a little longer.

Let the gateau cool before removing from the tin and putting onto a plate to serve.

Chocolate hazelnut brownies ▾

Serves 6
(Makes 24 brownies)
PREPARATION TIME: 30 minutes
COOKING TIME: about 30 minutes

125g/4½oz shelled
blanched hazelnuts
250g/9oz rich dark chocolate
2 eggs
200g/7oz caster sugar
½ tbsp vanilla sugar
125g/4½oz butter +
some for the tin
1 pinch salt
100g/4oz flour +
some for the tin
1 tsp baking powder

Preheat oven to Gas 6/ 200°C/fan oven180°C. Butter and flour an 20cm/8in square tin.

Dry-fry the hazelnuts for a few minutes, shaking the pan to brown evenly. Set aside.

Break the chocolate into small pieces, melt in a pudding basin or heatproof bowl, either in the microwave (1 minute on full power) or in a bain-marie. When it has completely softened, remove from the fire and lightly stir with a spatula.

Beat the eggs, caster sugar, vanilla sugar, salt and lightly melted butter together in a bowl with an electric whisk. When it is evenly mixed, add the flour, baking powder, chocolate and the chopped hazelnuts. Stir with a wooden spoon. Tip the mixture into a tin, smoothing the surface.

Place in the middle of the oven for about 40 minutes until the surface turns a rich dark brown. Check that cooking is finished by inserting a knife: the blade should come out dried. If it doesn't, continue cooking for a little longer.

When finished, remove the bake from the oven and turn out onto a wire rack. Leave until completely cooled before cutting into twenty-four squares.

Serve the brownies on a large plate.

[Buttercream.]

Buttercream is used for decorating, filling and decorating Genoese sponges, sponge fingers, Yule logs and uncooked gateaux made with sponge biscuits. To make successful buttercream, leave the yolk and syrup mixture to cool to room temperature before adding it to the butter, otherwise the butter may melt.

Buttercream is perishable: it should be stored in the fridge for no longer than 12 hours.

Traditional French buttercream

To decorate a gateau serving 6 to 8
250g/9oz sugar lumps
200ml/7fl oz water
8 egg yolks
1 pinch of salt
250g/9oz unsalted butter
Optional flavourings: 1 tbsp vanilla or coffee extract, 2 level tbsp cocoa, powdered praline, alcohol or liqueur (rum, kirsch, orange liqueur)

Preparation
Make a simple sugar syrup with the sugar lumps and water and heat until it forms a thread (see p.15). Lightly whisk the yolks and salt. Continue beating while slowly adding the boiling syrup. Cream the butter (do not melt): it should be soft and well beaten. Slowly add the egg mixture to the butter, beating well until it forms a firm shiny cream. Flavour as desired.

Easy buttercream

To fill a 26cm/10in gateau (serves 6 to 8)
2 medium eggs
250g/9oz caster sugar
250g/9oz butter
Optional flavouring

Preparation
Break the eggs into a small pan; sprinkle the sugar over the top and place on a low heat. Work with a spatula until the sugar dissolves: there should be no granulation. Leave the mixture to cool, stirring frequently. Dice the butter and beat to a cream (but do not melt) using the wooden spoon. Once the egg and sugar mix has completely cooled, add the butter, a little at a time, while continuing to beat. When the cream becomes smooth and homogenous, add your chosen flavouring.

Chocolate buttercream for decorating and filling

To fill a 26cm/10in gateau (serves 6 to 8)
75g/3oz rich dark chocolate
60g/2½oz butter
30g/1¼oz icing sugar
1 egg

Preparation
Melt the chocolate in a bain-marie. Cream the butter in a bowl. Add the other ingredients to the butter and mix using a spatula.

Easter torte

Serves 8
PREPARATION TIME: 1 hour
COOKING TIME: 30–40 minutes

GENOESE SPONGE
5 eggs
250g/9oz caster sugar
250g/9oz plain flour
20g/¾oz butter
for greasing the tin

COFFEE BUTTERCREAM
2 eggs + 1 yolk
250g/9oz caster sugar
250g/9oz butter
2 tbsp coffee extract

ICING
200g/7oz icing sugar
2 or 3 tbsp very strong coffee

DECORATION
Mini Easter eggs and chocolate-
covered coffee beans

Make the Genoese sponge: break the eggs into a bowl placed over a pan of simmering water. Add the caster sugar and beat with an electric whisk until the mixture forms a pale mousse. Remove from the heat, sprinkle the flour on top and fold it in carefully.

Lightly butter a deep 25cm/10in sandwich tin and fill with the mixture. Bake in the middle of the oven for 30 minutes. Test the cake with a skewer or knife. When it is ready, the skewer or knife will come out dry, without the mixture clinging to it. Extend the cooking by 10 minutes if necessary. Take the sponge out of the oven and turn it out onto a wire rack to cool.

Make the coffee buttercream: beat the eggs and the yolk with the caster sugar until the mixture is thick enough to leave a ribbon trail on top. Add the butter in small pieces. Beat vigourously until the mixture becomes creamy then add the coffee extract. Chill until ready to use.

When the Genoese sponge has completely cooled, slice horizontally into three equal layers. Place one of these (which will form the base of the dessert) on a round serving plate and spread half of the buttercream over it. Place the second layer on top and spread with the remaining butter-cream. Place the last layer on top to form the gateau.

Make the icing: Moisten the icing sugar with the coffee until the mixture is smooth and shiny. If it is too thick, add a few more drops of coffee. If too runny, add a little more icing sugar. Using a flexible spatula spread the icing over the top and sides of the gateau. Decorate immediately with the mini eggs and chocolate covered coffee beans. Leave to set before serving.

Chestnut log

Serves 8

PREPARATION TIME: 45 minutes
plus chilling time
COOKING TIME: 10–12 minutes

SYRUP
200g/7oz caster sugar
200ml/7fl oz water
4 tbsp cognac

BISCUIT
8 eggs
330g/10½oz caster sugar
200g/7oz sifted plain flour
20g/¾oz butter
for greasing the tin

CHESTNUT CREAM FOR FILLING
250g/9oz butter
500g/1lb 2oz sweetened
chestnut purée with vanilla
4 tbsp cognac

DECORATION
Small Christmas cake
decorations (optional)
Small meringue mushrooms
(optional)
Glacé chestnuts (optional)

Make the syrup: put the caster sugar and water in a pan and simmer over a medium heat until the mixture reaches a syrupy consistency. Do not let the syrup change colour. Remove from the heat add the cognac (do this carefully – the mixture may spit) and cool.

Preheat oven to Gas 7/220°C/fan oven 200°C

Make the biscuit: separate the egg whites and yolks. Cream the yolks and the caster sugar in a bowl until thick. Beat the whites until they stand in stiff peaks. Delicately incorporate them into the yolk mixture, alternating with the flour.

Butter a 20cm/8in x 30cm/12in shallow rectangular tin. Spread the mixture evenly on it. Place in the middle of the oven for 10–12 minutes: the biscuit should be flexible and pale yellow.

Remove from the oven and turn the biscuit onto a clean damp cloth. Moisten immediately with the syrup. Roll the biscuit on itself and keep in the cloth until it has completely cooled.

Make the chestnut cream filling: beat the butter in the mixer until it forms a creamy paste. Add the chestnut purée and the cognac, and work until the cream is perfectly blended.

Unroll the biscuit. Evenly spread with two thirds of the chestnut cream. Roll it up again and place on a plate with the end underneath. Cover the whole log with the remaining cream. Use the back of a fork to draw lines on the log to simulate bark. Chill for at least 12 hours for the cream to set. Just before serving, decorate with the small Christmas cake decorations, meringue mushrooms and the glace chestnuts.

VARIATION: To make a chocolate flavoured biscuit, add two tablespoons of cocoa to the flour.

Summer fruit gateau

Serves 8

PREPARATION TIME: 1 hour 30 minutes, plus chilling time

500g/1lb 2oz strawberries
250g/9oz redcurrants
1 x 20cm/8in Genoese sponge

SYRUP
250g/9oz caster sugar
25ml/1fl oz water
1 tbsp kirsch

MERINGUE BUTTER CREAM
3 egg whites
200g/7oz caster sugar
1 pinch of salt
20g/¾oz butter
2 tbsp kirsch

DECORATION
250g/9oz raspberry jelly
a few raspberries, cherries,
redcurrants, white currants

Make the syrup: put the caster sugar into a pan with the water and simmer, stirring with a spatula until the sugar has completely dissolved. Leave on a medium heat for about 6 minutes (to produce a clear coloured syrupy consistency). Remove from the heat, add the kirsch and set aside.

Make meringue buttercream: put the egg whites into a bowl with the caster sugar and salt. Put the bowl over a pan of hot water and beat the sugar and egg whites with an electric whisk until they form a thick, firm shining mousse. Leave to cool. Cream the butter. Add the kirsch then, little by little, delicately fold in the cold meringue.

Wash and dry the strawberries and remove the stalks. Keep a dozen to one side for decoration and slice the others in two from top to bottom. Wash the redcurrants and remove separate from the stems.

Using a sharp (or electric) knife, slice the Genoese sponge into three equal disks. Place one to form the base on a cake plate. Using a brush, moisten with the kirsch syrup, then spread with a layer of cream about 1.5cm/⅝in thick.

Alternate the halved strawberries and redcurrants. Begin at the edges, showing the sliced part of the strawberries. Cover with the second layer of cake, moisten and garnish with the remaining cream and fruits. Set the third piece of cake on top. Carefully align and balance the sides of the gateau for good presentation.

Place the gateau in the fridge for an hour to firm. If necessary, soften the raspberry jelly by mixing with a little kirsch and cover the top of the gateau. Slice the reserved strawberries and decorate with these and the other fruits. Serve the summer fruit gateau chilled but not frozen.

[Custard]

The perfect accompaniment for brioches, pound cake, Genoese sponges, and floating islands, custard is also used as a sauce with puddings, rice gateaux, charlottes and even for making ice cream.

Serves 6
1litre/1¾ pints milk
Flavourings as desired: vanilla pod, coffee extract, chocolate or caramel
6 egg yolks
125g/4½oz caster sugar

Preparation
Bring the milk to the boil and add the vanilla pod, sliced lengthways in two, or other flavouring. Infuse for a few minutes and remove. Put the egg yolks into a large mixing bowl and sprinkle over the sugar. Beat with the spatula until the mixture forms a thick creamy mousse. Continue to stir while adding the hot milk in small quantities so as not to scramble the egg. Tip into a pan and place on a low heat to thicken, stirring continuously, being careful not to allow the mixture to boil (if it gets too hot, the cream 'turns', becoming like scrambled egg; if this should happen, tip it immediately into a cold bowl, let it cool and beat vigourously with an electric mixer or an egg whisk). When the froth has completely gone and the cream thickens to coat a spoon that is dipped in it, the custard is ready. Pour it into a cold bowl or jug to stop it continuing to cook.

Storage
Custard keeps for up to 12 hours if chilled in the fridge.

Figs with almond cream ›

Serves 4

PREPARATION TIME: 20 minutes
COOKING TIME: 15 minutes

8 fresh figs

CUSTARD
500ml/18fl oz milk
1 vanilla pod
4 egg yolks
60g/2½oz caster sugar
2 drops of bitter almond extract

WHIPPING CREAM
225ml/8fl oz single
or whipping cream
50g/2oz icing sugar
2 drops of bitter almond extract

DECORATION
50g/2oz flaked almonds

Make custard **(see p. 81)**. Add the almond extract after the custard has cooled and place in the fridge.

Wash the figs and cut into quarters not cutting all the way through the base of the figs. Pinch the base to open out the figs into 'flowers'.

Make the whipping cream **(see p. 95)** adding the almond extract at the same time as the sugar. Fill an icing bag with a 1cm/½in plain or fluted nozzle and pipe into the centre of each fig. Keep in the fridge until needed. Just before serving, garnish the bowls filled with custard by placing two cream-filled figs in each and decorate with flaked almonds.

Chocolate marquise

Serves 8 to 10

PREPARATION TIME: 45 minutes,
plus chilling overnight
COOKING TIME: about 15 minutes

MARQUISE
250g/9oz rich dark chocolate
3 tbsp water
125g/4½oz butter +
a little for the tin
3 eggs
100g/4oz icing sugar
A few drops of vanilla
or coffee extract

CUSTARD
250ml/9fl oz milk
2 egg yolks
50g/2oz caster sugar
A few drops of vanilla
or coffee extract

DECORATION
Chocolate chips or grains

Make the marquise: melt the chocolate in a pan set over a simmering pan of water (or in the microwave). Remove from the heat.

Cream the butter. Separate the egg yolks from the whites. Beat the egg whites until stiff.

Beat the yolks, one at a time, into the butter. Add the icing sugar (sieve if there are any lumps) and beat well. Add the melted chocolate, then the vanilla essence or coffee extract, and beat for a while. Leave to cool completely before adding the beaten egg whites.

Butter a 17cm/6¾in diameter ceramic or glass mould and fill with the mixture. Place in the fridge overnight.

Make the custard: bring the milk to the boil. Beat the egg yolks and caster sugar until the mixture turns a creamy white. Add to the boiling milk and thicken over a low heat, stirring continuously. Remove from the heat before it boils, when it is thick enough to coat the spoon. Leave to cool. Add the vanilla essence or coffee extract.

To remove from the mould, place the mould in hot water for a few seconds then upend it on a plate. Decorate the marquise with chocolate chips and serve with the custard.

Floating islands

Serves 6 to 8
PREPARATION TIME: 25 minutes
COOKING TIME: 10 minutes

CUSTARD
1 litre/1¾ pints milk
1 vanilla pod
6 egg yolks
250g/9oz caster sugar

CARAMEL
15 sugar lumps
a little water

ISLAND
6 egg whites
1 pinch of salt

Make a custard **(see p. 81)**, keeping the egg whites to one side in a separate bowl.

Make a pale yellow caramel by heating the sugar lumps moistened with water **(see p. 16)**.

Meanwhile, make the islands: beat the egg whites and salt until stiff. Fill a large pan with water and bring to the boil. Using two soup or tablespoons, scoop up spoonfuls of egg white and poach in the boiling water. Take them out, set on kitchen paper and leave to drip dry. Pour the cold custard into a large shallow dish. Arrange the egg whites on the surface. Decorate with spun sugar **(see p. 15)** made from sugar and water syrup and eat at once.

‹ Bavarian cream

Serves 6
PREPARATION TIME: 45 minutes,
plus chilling time
COOKING TIME: 20 minutes

1 vanilla pod
250ml/9fl oz milk
3 egg yolks
250g/9oz caster sugar
6 gelatine leaves
250ml/9fl oz crème fraîche
or double cream
400g/14oz raspberries
50ml/2fl oz raspberry brandy
(optional)

Whip the cream and put in the fridge.

Split the vanilla pod in two, add to the milk and bring to the boil. Infuse for 10 minutes, and then remove the vanilla pod.

Beat the egg yolks with 125g/4½oz of the sugar in a mixing bowl until the mixture forms a thick creamy mousse. Gently pour in the hot milk while stirring. Tip the mixture back into the pan and, still stirring, thicken over a low heat. Remove from the heat at the first sign of simmering.

Soften the gelatine for a few minutes in a bowl of cold water. Wipe dry and melt in the hot cream. Strain the cream through a sieve and leave to cool, stirring from time to time to prevent it forming a skin. When it is cold, add the whipped cream.

Choose a 20cm/8in mould. Pass under cold water, fill with the mixture, keeping it level, and place in the fridge for 6 hours.

Prepare the raspberries **(see p. 18)**. Keep back 100g/4oz to decorate and purée the rest in a liquidizer or food processor. Add the remaining sugar and the raspberry brandy as desired.

To serve, remove the cream from the mould by dipping it in warm water for one minute and then inverting onto a serving plate. Decorate with the reserved raspberries. Serve the sauce separately.

[Patisserie

cream]

Patisserie cream is used to garnish the base of tarts, to fill gateaux and crêpes and to prepare a variety of creamy puddings.

Adding ground almonds at the end of cooking, makes almond or marzipan cream. The best advice for making successful patisserie cream is to avoid lumps forming and cream sticking during cooking. Cook your mixture very slowly and stir continuously, not forgetting the sides and bottom of the pan.

Makes 1 litre/1¾ pints milk
2 whole eggs + 4 yolks (or 4 whole eggs to make a thicker cream)
250g/9oz caster sugar
125g/4½oz flour
1 litre/1¾ pints milk
Optional flavourings: vanilla, chocolate, coffee, caramel...

Preparation
Beat the eggs and caster sugar together, using a spatula, until the mixture turns creamy white. Fold the flour into the mixture, then continue stirring. Gradually add the hot flavoured milk. Pour the mixture into a pan and cook on a low heat while continuing to stir. Remove from the heat at the first sign of simmering. Sprinkle with caster sugar to prevent it forming a skin as it cools.

Storage
Patisserie cream keeps for up to 12 hours in the fridge.

Strawberry meringue gateau ⏷

Serves 8
PREPARATION TIME: 40 minutes
COOKING TIME: 5 minutes

300g/10oz ripe scented
strawberries or
wild strawberries
1 Genoese sponge cake:
either 20cm/8in square or
23cm/9in round

KIRSCH PATISSERIE CREAM
1 egg + 2 yolks
80g/3¾oz caster sugar
50g/2oz cornflour
500ml/18fl oz milk
1 tbsp kirsch
80g/3¾ butter

KIRSCH SYRUP
125ml/4fl oz water
125g/4½oz caster sugar
3 tbsp kirsch

MERINGUE
1 egg white
50g/2oz caster sugar
Pinch of salt

Make the patisserie cream **(see p. 87)**: add the kirsch and the diced butter after removing the cream from the heat. Stir occasionally as the cream cools.

Make the syrup: heat the water and caster sugar in a pan and boil for 1 minute. Cool and add the kirsch.

Wash and dry the strawberries and remove the stalks. Leave whole if small, otherwise slice them. Keep a few whole ones to decorate.

Make the meringue: put the egg white, caster sugar and salt in a bowl over a bain-marie. Beat with an electric beater until the mixture is smooth thick white and shiny.

Preheat oven to Gas 9/240°C/fan oven 220°C. Slice the sponge into two layers. Place one layer onto a baking sheet. Use a pastry brush to moisten with the kirsch syrup. Spread with a thick layer of patisserie cream. Cover wiht strawberries, pushing them into the cream. Place the second layer on top and moisten with the syrup. Cover the meringue gateau completely with the cream, using a spatula to smooth the surface.

Place in the oven for 5 minutes to lightly brown the meringue, then draw marks over the top using a red-hot fork or skewer. Carefully transfer to a serving plate and decorate with a few sliced strawberries on top of the gateau before serving.

Neapolitan sponge cake

Serves 6

PREPARATION TIME: 50 minutes
COOKING TIME: 45 minutes

GENOESE SPONGE
4 eggs
125g/4½oz caster sugar
100g/4oz/4oz sieved flour +
extra for the tin
60g/2½oz melted butter +
extra for the tin

PATISSERIE CREAM WITH
CANDIED FRUITS
3 egg yolks
100g/4oz caster sugar
50g/2oz flour
500ml/18fl oz milk
250g/9oz chopped candied fruits
1 liqueur glass kirsch or
2 liqueur glasses maraschino
(about 50ml/2fl oz)

SYRUP
1 glass water (100ml/3½fl oz)
50g/2oz sugar lumps
1 glass port or kirsch or 2
glasses maraschino (about
100ml/3½fl oz)

MERINGUE
3 egg whites
100g/4oz caster sugar

DECORATION
Glacé cherries
Angelica stems

Make the candied fruits the day before: chop and macerate in your chosen alcohol, cover and set aside at room temperature.

Next day, make the Genoese sponge: preheat the oven to Gas 6/200°C/fan oven 180°C. Put the whole eggs and caster sugar into a bowl and whisk over a pan of simmering water with an electric whisk until the mixture is thick and creamy and has doubled in volume. Remove from the heat and quickly add the flour and the butter, using a wooden spoon. Butter and flour a 20cm/8in cake tin, fill with the mixture and bake for 30 minutes.

Meanwhile, make the patisserie cream: beat the egg yolks and caster sugar until the mixture is pale, sift the flour on top and mix together with two tablespoons of cold milk. Put the remaining milk in a pan and bring to the boil, pouring gently onto the mixture. Return the mixture to the pan and heat to thicken, stirring constantly with a wooden spoon. Do not boil. Leave to cool, then add the macerated candied fruit.

Make the syrup: boil the water and sugar lumps until the sugar has dissolved and the syrup is thickened slightly – it should not change colour Remove from the heat and add your chosen alcohol.

Make the meringue: beat the egg whites until stiff, add the caster sugar and beat for a few minutes longer. Lower the oven temperature to Gas 4/ 180°C/ fan oven 160°C. Slice the gateau into two equal layers and put the base onto the bottom of a removable tart tin or baking sheet. Moisten with half of the syrup and spread the patisserie cream over it with a spatula. Put the top half of the gateau on top and sprinkle with the remaining syrup. Cover the gateau with the meringue mixture, using a spatula. Arrange a few glacé cherries and pieces of angelica on top to decorate. Bake for 15 minutes until crisp and a light golden colour. Serve cold.

Fresh fig gateau

Serves 8
PREPARATION TIME: 1 hour,
plus chilling time
COOKING TIME: 20–25 minutes

GENOESE SPONGE
4 eggs
125g/4½oz caster sugar
pinch of salt
125g/4½oz flour +
extra to flour the tin
60g/2½oz melted butter +
extra for the tin

FIG PATISSERIE CREAM
1 egg + 2 yolks
80g/3oz caster sugar
30g/1¼oz plain flour
20g/¾oz cornflour
400ml/14fl oz whole milk
½ vanilla pod
2 gelatine leaves
2 tbsp dessert wine
6 purple figs

DECORATION
3 tbsp fig jam
1 tbsp dessert wine
2 figs
Orange zest (optional)

Make the sponge. Break the eggs into a bowl, adding the sugar and salt. Place the bowl on top of a pan of hot water on a gentle heat (do not let the water boil). Whisk until the mixture thickens, trebles in volume and turns pale yellow. Remove the bowl from the hot water.

Preheat oven to Gas 6/200°C/fan oven 180°C. Sift the flour onto the surface of the mixture and gently fold in using a spatula. Add the melted butter and finish mixing as quickly and lightly as possible: the mixture should remain light and full of air.

Butter and flour a deep 20cm/8in sandwich tin and fill with the mixture. Bake in the middle of the oven for 20 minutes. Check that the cake is ready by inserting the tip of a knife or a metal skewer: it should come out clean. If necessary, extend the cooking time by a few minutes. Turn the sponge out onto a wire rack and leave to cool.

Prepare the patisserie cream. Soak the gelatine in a bowl of cold water. Heat the dessert wine in a small pan, squeeze out and dissolve the gelatine. Mix with the patisserie cream and transfer to a large well chilled, shallow dish. When the cream has cooled slightly, put it in the fridge for 2 hours. Peel and roughly chop the figs. When the cream is cold, add the figs to the mixture, replacing in the fridge until needed.

Slice the sponge in two. Place the bottom half on a serving plate and spread with the patisserie cream. Place the other half on top.

Prepare the decorative icing: Mix the jam and the dessert wine. Spread it over the top of the gateau, taking care not to let it run down the sides.

Keep the fig sponge in the fridge until serving. Just before serving, wash and finely slice the remaining figs, arranging them on the gateau and all around the plate. Finally garnish with the orange rind.

Andalusian gateau

Serves 8

PREPARATION TIME: 40 minutes
COOKING TIME: 20–30 minutes

250g/9oz caster sugar
250ml/9fl oz water
2 unwaxed oranges
125g/4½oz flaked almonds
6 tbsp apricot jam
50ml/2fl oz orange liqueur
1 x 24cm/9in Genoese
sponge cake

PATISSERIE CREAM
250ml/9fl oz milk
1 whole egg + 1 yolk
50g/2oz caster sugar +
1 tbsp for the top
2 tbsp cornflour

Place the caster sugar and water in a large pan and heat gently until the sugar has dissolved. Scrub the oranges thoroughly, slice and put in the sugar syrup. Simmer lightly for 20–30 minutes and leave to cool in the syrup.

Make the patisserie cream: warm the milk. Whisk the egg, the yolk and the caster sugar together in a bowl until creamy. Add the cornflour and dissolve with the warm milk. Pour the mixture into a pan and thicken over a gentle heat, stirring continuously with a wooden spoon. Remove from the heat and pour into a bowl. Sprinkle with the spoonful of caster sugar to prevent a skin forming on the surface and set aside to cool.

Spread the almonds over a baking sheet and toast in the top of the oven (or dry-roast in a non-stick frying pan without oil). Set aside.

Spoon the apricot jam into a pan and heat gently to make it runny. Add two or three tablespoons of the orange syrup to make it more liquid if needed. Remove from the heat. Add the orange liqueur to 100ml/3½fl oz of the orange syrup.

Add a tablespoon of the orange syrup to the patisserie cream.

Slice the Genoese sponge in half. Place the bottom onto a plate. Moisten with half of the orange liqueur syrup. Sprinkle the rest over the other half. Spread the cream over the base of the gateau and place the upper half on top. Brush the surface of the gateau with the jam and arrange the orange slices on top. Spread jam on the sides to make the toasted almonds stick to them. Chill until just before serving.

Strawberry and pistachio tart

Serves 8

PREPARATION TIME: 30 minutes
COOKING TIME: 20 minutes

300g/10oz shortcrust pastry

PATISSERIE CREAM
2 eggs
50g/2oz caster sugar
1 sachet vanilla sugar
30g/1¼oz potato flour
250ml/9fl oz milk
20g/¾oz butter
125g/4½oz unsalted broken or
whole shelled pistachios

FILLING
500g/1lb 2oz strawberries
1 tbsp redcurrant jelly
1 tbsp kirsch

Preheat oven to Gas 8/230°C/fan oven 210°C. Roll the pastry out on a lightly floured surface to 3mm/⅛in thick and use to line a 26cm/10½in tart tin. Make a pretty edge by doubling over the pastry and pinching all the way round the edge with the thumbs and forefingers. Cover the base with greaseproof paper and baking beans and bake for about 20 minutes until the edges of the pastry turn golden brown.

Make the patisserie cream **(see p. 87)**. Remove from the heat, add the butter cut into small pieces to prevent a thick skin forming, and 100g/4oz of the broken pistachios. Leave to cool. Remove the paper and beans from the tart. Spread the pistachio patisserie cream into the base.

Wash the strawberries and remove the stems. Slice in two, and arrange cut side down on the cream. Dissolve the redcurrant jelly in the kirsch, spread over the strawberries and sprinkle the remaining pistachios over the top. Turn out onto a round plate before serving.

[Whipped

cream]

Chantilly or French whipping cream is ideal for decorating ice cream, gateaux, creams and tarts as well as for filling choux pastries, Saint-Honoré gateaux, savarins, charlottes, meringues and other desserts. It also makes a lovely accompaniment for red fruits and drained fruits preserved in syrup. When making French whipped cream, follow these basic hints:
- The cream should be fresh and very cold; choose a rounded bowl if you are whisking it by hand and a tall narrow container if you are using an electric whisk. In warm weather, this will need to have been previously cooled in the fridge; if it is very hot, set the cooled bowl over a bowlful of ice cubes to whip the cream.
- For best results, use icing sugar, which is finer and lighter, rather than caster sugar, to sweeten.

Serves 4 to 6
250ml/9fl oz chilled single, whipping or
  UHT cream
50g/2oz icing sugar
½–1 tbsp vanilla sugar

Preparation
Add the icing sugar and vanilla (or vanilla sugar) to the cream. Whip the mixture, using a hand whisk if possible, slowly at first and then more quickly, checking the consistency of the cream. Stop beating as soon as the frothy cream becomes firm enough to form a peak on the end of the whisk, and when marks from the whisk remain on the surface.

Storing
Whipped cream keeps for about one hour if chilled in the fridge (any longer and it will collapse)..

Coffee meringue gateau

Serves 6 to 8
PREPARATION TIME: 35 minutes
COOKING TIME: 4 hours

GATEAU
2 egg whites
50g/2oz caster sugar
50g/2oz icing sugar
2 tsp instant coffee

FILLING
225ml/8fl oz crème fraîche
30g/1¼oz icing sugar
2 tbsp whiskey (optional)

Preheat the oven to Gas ½/120°C/fan oven 100°C.

Make the meringue gateau: beat the egg whites. As soon as they have increased in volume (but before they have become stiff), sprinkle the caster sugar over and continue beating until firm. Mix together the icing sugar and instant coffee and add gently to the mousse.

Draw two 18cm/7in circles on buttered baking paper and using a flexible spatula, carefully spread the meringue mixture over the inside of the circles. Put the rest of the meringue into a piping bag with a wide nozzle and pipe along the edges of the circles. Cook for 4 hours, heating the oven for just 15 minutes each hour, and turning it off for the remaining 45 minutes, and so on. When cooked, place on a cold surface immediately (such as marble) then remove the paper. Set aside to cool completely.

Make the filling: whip the crème fraîche and icing sugar by hand, adding the whiskey to the mixture at the end.

Spread a layer of cream on one of the meringue circles and cover with the second. Use an icing bag to pipe five cream rosettes in the middle before serving.

Redcurrant amandine gateau ›

Serves 6
PREPARATION TIME: 40 minutes,
plus chilling time
COOKING TIME: 25 minutes

225ml/8fl oz single or
whipping cream
30g/1¼oz icing sugar
500g/1lb 2oz redcurrants
2 tbsp redcurrant jelly

AMANDINE GATEAU
250g/9oz butter +
some for the tin
250g/9oz caster sugar
3 eggs
100g/4oz flour
50g/2oz ground almonds

Preheat oven to Gas 6/200°C/fan oven 180°C. Make the amandine gateau: Cream the butter, add the sugar and beat until smooth. Continue beating and add the eggs one by one. Sprinkle the flour over and fold in the ground almonds.

Butter 2 x 20cm/8in sandwich tins and divide the mixture between them. Bake for 25 minutes. Remove from the oven and turn the cakes out onto a wire rack to cool.

Whip the cream and icing sugar together. **(see p. 95)**. Wash and dry the redcurrants. Remove the fruit from the stalks and mix with the redcurrant jelly.

Spread two-thirds of the cream onto the first cake. Sprinkle with the redcurrants. Set the second cake on top. Use a piping bag to form a ring of cream curls. Arrange the remaining redcurrants in the middle. Chill for 1 hour in the fridge before serving.

Small coffee pots

Serves 4

PREPARATION TIME: 10 minutes
COOKING TIME: 3-5 minutes

3 eggs
1 tsp instant coffee
1 tbsp hot water
25g/1oz butter
4 tbsp caster sugar
1 tbsp golden rum
1 tsp coffee essence
50ml/2fl oz single crème fraîche
or whipping cream
1 tbsp icing sugar
Shelled walnuts

Break the eggs and separate the whites and yolks into separate bowls. Dissolve the coffee in the hot water.

Add the butter, caster sugar, rum, coffee, coffee essence to the egg yolks and place over a pan of simmering water. Beat for 3-5 minutes, until the mixture thickens. Remove from the heat and stand the bowl in a larger bowl filled with cold water.

Whip the egg whites until stiff and stir in the coffee mixture, spoonful by spoonful, continuing to beat. Divide the mixture between four ramekins.

Whip the cream, adding the icing sugar to sweeten. Just before serving, garnish the ramekins with spoonfuls of whipping cream and decorate with the roughly chopped walnuts. Serve chilled.

Fromage blanc with raspberry coulis ›

Serves 4

PREPARATION TIME: 15 minutes
COOKING TIME: 1 hour

500g/1lb 2oz fromage blanc

RASPBERRY COULIS
300g/10oz fresh or frozen
raspberries (thawed if frozen)
50g/2oz caster sugar
juice of 1 lemon

WHIPPED CREAM
225ml/8fl oz fresh
whipping cream
2 tbsp icing sugar
½ tbsp vanilla sugar

DECORATION
16 raspberries

Put the fromage blanc in a sieve and leave to drain for 1 hour.

Make the raspberry coulis: hull any fruits if necessary and roll in a damp cloth to clean. Combine with the caster sugar and lemon juice and blend until smooth. (sieve if you wish to remove the seeds). Chill until ready to use.

Make the whipping cream **(see p. 95)**.

Empty the fromage blanc into a mixing bowl, stir lightly with a fork and fold in the whipped cream. Divide the mixture between 4 individual glasses or bowls and chill until ready to use. Just before serving, remove from the fridge and decorate with four raspberries each. Serve the chilled coulis separately.

Exotic Puits d'Amour

Serves 4
PREPARATION TIME: 15 minutes

4 bananas
Juice of 1 lemon
4 round slices pineapple
30g/1¼oz caster sugar
225ml/8fl oz crème fraîche, UHT
or whipping cream
2 tbsp icing sugar
1 tbsp shelled unsalted
pistachios
4 glace cherries

Peel two bananas and cut into thick round slices and sprinkle with half the lemon juice to stop them turning black. Place a pineapple slice, cut into small pieces and re made into a circle onto each of four small plates. Arrange a quarter of the banana slices, slightly overlapping over each of the four plates.

Peel and mash the remaining bananas with the remaining lemon juice and caster sugar. Whip the creme fraiche or cream, adding the icing sugar. Set aside two tablespoons of whipped cream. Fold the remaining cream gently into the mashed banana. Divide this cream between the four pineapple rounds, placing in the centre.

Scatter the roughly chopped pistachios over the edges. Top each puits off with whipping cream and garnish with a glace cherry. Serve chilled.

‹ Chocolate terrine with orange slivers

Serves 8
PREPARATION TIME: 30 minutes,
plus chilling overnight

200g/7oz whole candied
orange peel
4 tbsp Grand-Marnier
400g/14oz rich dark chocolate
2 tbsp water
250g/9oz unsalted butter
225ml/8fl oz crème fraîche, UHT
or whipping cream
40g/1¾oz icing sugar
125g/4½oz ground almonds

Cut the candied peel into strips 1 to 2cm/½-¾in long. Put in a bowl with the Grand-Marnier and set aside until needed, stirring from time to time.

Break the chocolate into squares in a bowl, add the water and melt over a pan of simmering water. Add the butter and stir to create a smooth paste. Cool.

Whip the cream, adding the icing sugar as it starts to form peaks. Gently fold into the chocolate mixture and fold in until just combined. Add the orange slivers with their Grand-Marnier juice and the ground almonds and stir until combined.

Line a rectangular cake tin, 14cm/5½in long, with cling film, generously overlapping the sides. Pour the mixture in and smooth the surface. Cover over with the overlapping cling film and place in the fridge for at least 12 hours or overnight.

Carefully turn out of the tin onto a serving dish, simply by pulling on the cling film and serve at once.

[Ice cream]

Thanks to freezers, ice cream has today become a simple dessert that is easy to make and store. It is easily transformed into a number of desserts, as flavoursome as they are varied. To make them successfully, the mixture needs to be cold before being frozen. If you don't have an ice cream or sorbet maker, remember that you will need to stir the mixture a few times as it freezes to prevent ice crystals from forming. It takes at least 3 hours to freeze an ice cream to a good consistency and 2 hours for sorbet. Take hard ice cream out of the freezer 10 or 15 minutes before eating. To serve ice cream if you do not have a special ice cream spoon use two soup or tablespoons to form a long ovals ice cream, use the second to slide it into the glass or dish; you can also make large scoops with a single spoon by scraping it along the top of the ice cream.

Ice cream and sorbets can be kept for 1 to 2 months in the freezer at − 24°C/ −−11°F.

Ice cream

Makes 1 litre/1¾ pints ice cream
500ml/18fl oz plain milk or milk with chocolate, coffee, vanilla, cinnamon, or rose petal flavouring
4 to 6 egg yolks
100 to 125g/4 to 4½oz caster sugar

Preparation
Make a custard with the flavoured milk, egg yolks and sugar **(see p. 81)**. Pass through a sieve and leave to cool. To make the ice cream more creamy, after cooling replace some of the milk with single cream or add whipped cream or smooth fromage blanc.

Fruit ice cream

It is easy to make fruit ice cream: you simply have to add pureed fruits to chilled plain or flavoured custard. Use 300g to 400g/10oz to 14oz of fruit puree to 1 litre/1¾ pints custard **(see p. 81)**. Although any kind of fruit can be used, they need to be prepared. Whatever fruits you choose for making ice cream, add lemon juice to them to prevent oxidation (they turn brown and then black).

When using ripe fruits or fruits with soft flesh (peaches, bananas, strawberries, raspberries, mangoes), simply blend the flesh to a fine puree after removing the skins, seeds or stones.

When you have decided to use hard-fleshed fresh fruits or dried fruits (apples, pears, apricots or plums), cook them in a little water, syrup or wine before pureeing.

When you use watery fruits (grapes, redcurrants, blackcurrants, or citrus fruits), extract the juice by juicing or pressing, or cook for 5 minutes, squeeze, and sieve the mixture.

Sorbets made with thick fruit puree

When using fruits follow the same advice for making sorbets as for fruit ice cream.

Makes 1l/1¾ pints sorbet
200g/7oz caster sugar
Juice of 1 lemon
4 tbsp water
700-800g (1lb 9oz-1lb 12oz) fruit puree

Preparation
Make a syrup with the sugar, lemon juice and water, boiling it for 2 to 3 mins **(see p. 15)**. Cool the syrup, and beat into the fruit puree.

Fruit juice sorbets
Or liquid puree

When preparing fruit for making sorbets, follow the same advice for making sorbets as for fruit ice cream. Sorbets made from fruit juice or puree use a stiffly beaten egg white added to the sorbet as it freezes to make it smooth and creamy.

Makes 1litre/1¾pints sorbet
700ml/1¼ pints fruit juice
375g/12oz preserving sugar

Preparation
Boil the fruit juice with the sugar for 5 minutes. You can use reduced fruit juice from fruit previously cooked in wine or syrup (peaches, pears). Serve the sorbet with the fruit.

Rhubarb ice cream ›

Serves 8
PREPARATION TIME: 30 minutes
plus macerating time and
freezing time
COOKING TIME: 20-25 minutes

500g/1lb 2oz rhubarb
100g/4oz granulated sugar

CUSTARD
700ml/1¼ pint milk
½ vanilla pod
6 egg yolks
250g/9oz caster sugar
225ml/8fl oz single cream

Make the custard (see p. 81). When it is cold, strain through a fine sieve to remove any small lumps. Stir in the cream. Put in the fridge until needed.

Make the rhubarb: peel the stems, removing the fine skin that covers them and chop into small pieces. Alternate layers of rhubarb and layers of the sugar in a bowl and leave to macerate for 2 hours.

Pour the contents of the bowl into a pan. Cook on a medium heat, stirring occasionally, for 20 minutes to form a compote. Let the mixture cool completely and then puree in a blender to make a thick coulis. Carefully stir this into the custard.

Pour the mixture into a sorbet or ice cream maker and place in the freezer for 3 to 4 hours as directed in the instructions. As soon as the ice cream begins to freeze, transfer into a container so it may be stored in the freezer until it is used.

To serve, divide into individual glasses or bowls accompanied by small biscuits.

Baked Alaska

Serves 8 to 10
PREPARATION TIME: 30 minutes
plus freezing time
COOKING TIME: 10 minutes

1litre/1/¾pints ice cream (vanilla,
chocolate, strawberry or rum
and raisin)
4 egg whites
200g/7oz icing sugar
1 tbsp vanilla sugar
One 18–20cm/7–8in sponge cake
4 tbsp rum

TO FLAMBÉ
3 tbsp rum
1 sugar lump

Choose a mixing bowl with same size top as the sponge. Pile the ice cream into the bowl, push down firmly and place in the freezer for 30 minutes to set.

Beat the egg whites with 150g/5oz of the icing sugar. When the meringue stiffens add the remaining icing sugar and the vanilla sugar. Continue beating until the mixture forms stiff white peaks.

Preheat oven to Gas 9/240°C/fan oven 220°C. Place the sponge on an ovenproof serving dish. Pour rum over. Put the bowl with the ice cream into warm water for 20 seconds, wipe dry and turn the ice cream out on top of the sponge. Cover the whole thing with the meringue making sure all of the ice cream and sponge are covered (if they aren't, the ice cream will melt). Bake for about 10 minutes for the meringue to brown lightly, watching that it doesn't burn. Just before serving, warm the rum and sugar lump in a pan. At the table, as you serve, light the alcohol, and pour over the baked Alaska.

Iced nougat with chicory coulis

Serves 8

PREPARATION TIME: 1 hour 30 plus freezing time

Iced nougat
75g/3oz raisins
1 liqueur glass orange liqueur (about 100ml/3½fl oz)
75g/3oz blanched almonds
50g/2oz walnut pieces
50g/2oz shelled unsalted pistachios
200g/7oz rich dark chocolate
250g/9oz butter
4 eggs
100g/4oz icing sugar

CHICORY COULIS
5 egg yolks
80g/3¼oz caster sugar
500ml/18fl oz milk
200ml/7fl oz single or whipping cream
2 tbsp chicory extract

Make the iced nougat: wash the raisins and leave to macerate in orange liqueur for 2 hours or overnight if you have time.

Finely chop the almonds, walnuts and pistachios. Lightly toast in a non-stick pan without oil. Cool.

Break the chocolate into pieces and melt over a pan of simmering water with the butter. Stir together to make a fluid cream. Break the eggs and separate the whites and yolks. Beat the yolks one by one into the chocolate and leave to cool.

Put the egg whites and icing sugar into a bowl over a pan of simmering water. Beat with an electric whisk until they form a stiff, shiny mousse.

Stir the nuts and raisins into the chocolate, and fold in the meringue. Put into a 24cm/9½in long loaf tin lined with baking paper and place in the freezer for 8 to 10 hours.

Make the chicory coulis: Beat the egg yolks and caster sugar. Heat the milk and cream. Continue beating and gradually pour the hot liquid onto the eggs. Pour into a pan and thicken over a low heat, stirring until the custard coats the spoon. Remove from the heat before it comes to the boil and add the chicory extract. Store the coulis in the fridge until serving.

Serve thoroughly chilled.

Put the nougat into the fridge 1 hour before serving. Turn out onto a rectangular dish and cut into slices.

◂ Orange tutti-frutti cups

Serves 4

PREPARATION TIME: 20 minutes

250g/9oz mixed candied fruits
50g/2oz candied orange peel
500ml/18fl oz vanilla ice cream
2 oranges, peeled
25g/1oz caster sugar
2 tbsp orange liqueur
50g/2oz icing sugar
½ tsp ground ginger
100ml/3¼fl oz single cream

Put the candied fruits and the orange peel into a blender and finely chop. Place the fruit and orange mixture in a shallow dish and use a fork to mix with the ice cream. Return this to the freezer until just before serving.

Chop the orange flesh into rough squares, and remove the pips, pith and any membranes. Put into a bowl with the caster sugar and orange liqueur. Mix together and keep in the fridge until required.

Mix the icing sugar and ginger together. Whip the chilled cream **(see p. 95)** adding the icing sugar mix at the last minute.

To serve, divide the ice cream into individual coupes or bowls, using two warm soup spoons to form shaped ovals. Divide the orange fruit salad equally between them and garnish with the ginger whipping cream. Serve immediately.

Iced cherry soufflé ◄

Serves 8

PREPARATION: 1 hour
FREEZING TIME: 3–4 hours
minimum
RESTING TIME IN THE FRIDGE: 1 hour
(before eating)

600g/1lb 5oz cherries
500ml/18fl oz crème fraîche
300g/10oz caster sugar
100ml/3¼fl oz water
3 egg whites
1 tbsp cherry liqueur (or kirsch)

Cut out a sheet of baking paper 60x10cm/25x4in and place around the outside of a 16cm/6¼in porcelain soufflé dish, extending the height. Fasten with sticky tape. Wash the cherries and remove the stalks.

Bring the caster sugar and water to the boil in a pan. Cook for 5 minutes to make the syrup more concentrated. Add the cherries and boil for 8 minutes. Let the cherries cool in the juice and then drain. Keep a dozen for decoration. Stone and blend the rest.

Reduce the cherry syrup to about half over a high heat. It should be thick without having caramelised: it is ready when a teaspoonful placed in a bowl of cold water remains in one piece and can be squeezed between your fingers.

Beat the egg whites until stiff in a large mixing bowl. Continue beating and pour the boiling syrup in a thin stream over the egg whites: The whites will thicken, becoming pink, shiny and stiffer. Leave to cool.

Whip the cold cream. Gently fold into the cold egg whites, whipped cream, cherry puree and liqueur keeping the mixture as light as possible. Pour the mixture into the prepared dish until level with the paper. Freeze for 3 to 4 minimum, and put in the fridge for 1 hour before serving. To serve, remove the paper and decorate with the reserved cherries.

Quick fruit ice cream log

Serves 6

PREPARATION TIME: 20 minutes,
plus freezing time
COOKING TIME: 15 minutes

1 vanilla pod
250g/9oz caster sugar
50ml/2fl oz water
1 unwaxed lemon
1 small pineapple
1 mango
2 kiwis
1 orange (or 2 mandarins)
500ml/18fl oz vanilla ice cream
500ml/18fl oz mango-passion
fruit sorbet
12 dates
50g/2oz shelled unsalted
pistachios
3 tbsp icing sugar
Candied lemon slices (optional)

Make the syrup: split a vanilla pod and scrape out the seeds with a sharp knife and add to a pan with the pod and caster sugar, water, finely grated zest and juice of the lemon. Bring to a simmer, stirring until the sugar has completely dissolved. Continue cooking on a medium heat to obtain a syrupy consistency (about 8 minutes), without letting the mixture change colour. Discard the vanilla pod.

Peel the pineapple, mango and kiwis (cut three or four slices of kiwi and set aside for decoration). Chop the peeled fruits into small pieces, cut the orange into open segments (or quarter the mandarins) (keep some aside for decoration). Put the fruits into the syrup and poach for 5 mins.

Take the pan off the heat and let the fruits cool in the syrup: tip them all into a container placed inside a larger container filled with ice cubes to speed up the cooling process.

Take the vanilla ice cream and the mango-passion fruit sorbet out of the freezer and set aside until they begin to soften. Stone the dates and chop into small pieces. Carefully drain the fruits (put the syrup into a small bottle and store in the fridge for use in another dessert). Carefully combine the vanilla ice cream, the mango-passion fruit sorbet, the poached fruit, the finely chopped dates, and the roughly chopped pistachio nuts together in a mixing bowl.

Pour into a 18cm/7in long rectangular loaf tin and freeze for 1 hour then place in the middle of double thickness aluminium foil, and shape to form a log (or simply leave in the tin).

To serve, place (or turn out) onto a plate and cover with icing sugar. Cut the kiwi slices in half and arrange on the log. Arrange the reserved orange pieces with the candied lemon slices around. Serve chilled.

Individual orange sorbets

Serves 6

<small>PREPARATION TIME: 1 hour, plus freezing time</small>

7 large, unwaxed
thick-skinned oranges
40 sugar lumps
50ml/2fl oz mineral water
Juice of ½ lemon
1 egg white
1 tbsp icing sugar

Scrub the oranges thoroughly and dry them. Aromatise the sugar lumps by rubbing with the peel of one of the oranges and place in a pan with the water and lemon juice. Heat gently until the sugar dissolves. Leave to cool.

Remove the crowns of the other oranges by inserting the tip of a sharp knife two-thirds of the way up and making a series of intersecting 'V' cuts. Remove the flesh without damaging the skin: begin by cutting and removing a small cone shape then gradually remove the rest, keeping all the pulp and the juice to one side.

Squeeze or press the orange pulp to extract the juice. Filter and measure it: You will need 500ml/18fl oz (add the juice of the skinned orange to make up the quantity as required). Mix the orange juice and the chilled sugar syrup than freeze in an ice cream machine (if you do not have an ice cream machine place the mixture in the freezer). After freezing for 30 minutes, remove the mixture from the freezer, beat with a fork and refreeze.

Before it has completely frozen (about 1½ hours), beat the egg white until stiff, add the icing sugar and mix this until a thick glossy meringue is reached fold into the creamy frozen mixture. Replace in the freezer.

Carefully remove any white pith from the insides of the empty oranges and lids,. Place them in the freezer. To complete the garnish, remove the sorbet from the freezer and place in the fridge for 30 minutes to soften. Then spoon the sorbet into the skins, pressing down well. Place the crowns on top and return immediately to the freezer. Serve the individual orange sorbets on a plate.

Hot greengages with ice cream ›

Serves 4

<small>PREPARATION TIME: 35 minutes
COOKING TIME: 20-25 minutes
(depending on the ripeness of the fruit)</small>

500g/1lb 2oz greengages
100g/4oz granulated sugar
1 vanilla pod, split
1 unwaxed lemon
100ml/3½fl oz plum brandy
4 scoops of vanilla ice cream
1 sliced kiwi (optional)

Wash and the greengages and remove the stems. Slice in two and stone. Place in a pan with the granulated sugar, vanilla pod and finely grated rind and juice of the lemon. Cook on a low heat for 15 to 20 minutes with the lid on, stirring occasionally. When the mixture reaches compote consistency, add the plum brandy and mix. Cook for a few minutes longer then remove from the heat and divide between four dessert bowls or glasses.

Serve immediately with a scoop of vanilla ice cream in the centre. Decorate with the sliced kiwi as desired.

Candied fruit bombe

Serves 8 to 10
PREPARATION TIME: 1 hour,
plus chilling and freezing time

50g/2oz white raisins
50g/2oz currants
50g/2oz dried apricots
50g/2oz stoned dates
50g/2oz glace cherries
50g/2oz candied citron peel
50g/2oz candied orange peel
50g/2oz candied lemon peel
50g/2oz preserved angelica
50g/2oz flaked almonds
100ml/3¼fl oz cognac
4 eggs
200g/7oz caster sugar
400ml/14fl oz crème fraîche
Candied fruit to decorate

Chop all the dried and candied fruit finely. Toast the almonds in a non-stick pan without oil for 2 or 3 seconds.

Put the fruit and almonds into a mixing bowl and add the cognac. Stir, cover with cling film and place in the fridge for 2 hours.

Break the eggs into a bowl and beat with an electric beater until they thicken and become creamy. Gradually add the caster sugar and continue beating until the mixture turns shiny. Whip the cold cream in a bowl. Mix the two mixtures delicately together then add the fruit and maceration juices.

Line a round smooth bottomed salad bowl with cling film and pour the mixture into it. Cover with cling film and freeze for 12 hours. Just before serving remove the cling film from the top of bowl and carefully turn out the bombe onto a round plate. Remove the rest of the cling film. Decorate with candied fruit and tie a ribbon round the bottom of the bombe. Serve immediately.

Cassata

Serves 6
PREPARATION TIME: 1 hour,
plus freezing time

500ml/18fl oz vanilla ice cream
500ml/18fl oz chocolate
ice cream
250ml/9fl oz praline ice cream
100g/4oz caster sugar
3 tbsp water
2 egg whites
1 pinch of salt
100ml/3¼fl oz whipped cream
1 liqueur glass rum (about
100ml/3½fl oz)
100g/4oz diced candied fruit
1 tbsp blanched pistachios
chopped in half

Spoon vanilla ice cream into a very large mixing bowl, pressing down firmly to make a layer following the shape of the bowl. Freeze for 10 minutes. Follow the vanilla layer with a chocolate ice cream layer in the same bowl. Freeze again for 10 minutes and repeat using the praline ice cream. (The hole in the middle will contain the filling). Replace the bowl in the freezer until required.

Make the Italian meringue: put the caster sugar and water in a pan and boil, keeping a close watch: as it thickens, the syrup forms round bubbles that burst at the surface **("petit boulé", see p. 16)**. While the syrup is cooking beat the egg whites with the salt until stiff. Continue beating and pour the hot syrup in a thin stream over the eggs. Beat until cold.

Fold in the whipped cream, rum, candied fruit and pistachios. Fill the cavity in the bowl of ice cream with the mixture. Smooth the surface and cover with buttered baking paper. Freeze for a 3 hours minimum. To serve, remove the baking paper and turn the cassata out onto a round plate.

Rose ice cream ▲

Serves 4

PREPARATION TIME: 40 minutes,
plus freezing time
COOKING TIME: 15 minutes

500ml/18fl oz milk
Fresh untreated scented
rose petals
6 egg yolks
120g/3¾oz caster sugar
1 tbsp honey
50ml/2fl oz rose-flavoured syrup
24 candied Toulouse violets
200ml/7fl oz crème fraîche

Heat the milk on a low heat and add the rose petals. Remove from the heat as soon as it begins to simmer. Cover and leave to infuse for 30 minutes. Cream the egg yolks and caster sugar in a bowl. Stir in the cooled unfiltered milk. Rinse the pan, return the mixture to it and cook on a low heat stirring constantly with a wooden spoon to thicken the mixture until it coats the spoon; do not let it boil.

Pass through a sieve and stir in the honey. Set aside until cold. Add the rose flavoured syrup.

Roughly grind half of the candied violets, either in the blender or by placing in a cloth and crushing with the rolling pin. Add to the custard

Whip the cream until stiff and add to the cold custard mixture.

Pour into the ice cream maker. Freeze and beat for 2 to 3 hours depending on the instructions for your machine. To serve, use a scoop to divide the ice cream between glasses or coupes and decorate each with three candied violets. Serve at once.

COOK'S TIP

You can buy rose-flavoured syrup from an Indian or oriental grocers.

[Fruit

desserts]

Ripe natural fruit makes one of the simplest and most delicious desserts. But at any time of year, fruit can also be the main ingredient for making dishes in advance as well as creating many last minute desserts.
For recipes that use fruit only in season – you can make charlottes, salads, gratins, brochettes (kebabs) and fondues, making colourful use each of the fruits in turn as they appear in the markets or in your garden as the seasons progress. Some fruits are available all year round and enable you to make specific recipes at any time: bananas and coconuts and of course, apples, which are so delicious in tarts and can be used to make a variety of other things. Those that form compotes underpin a multitude of desserts ranging from the most simple to the most sophisticated and from the traditionally rustic to "new inventions". A wonderful way to profit from the riches fruit offers.

Fruit sabayon

Serves 4

PREPARATION TIME: 10 minutes
COOKING TIME: 15 minutes

500g/1lb 2oz seasonal fruit
2 eggs + 2 yolks
100g/4oz demerara sugar
50g/2oz flour
1 tsp vanilla sugar
100ml/3¼fl oz crème fraîche

Preheat oven to gas 6/200°C/fan oven 180°C.

Peel and dice the selected fruit, and spread them out on a small flat ovenproof dish.

Beat the eggs and yolks with the sugar, flour and vanilla in a mixing bowl set over a pan of simmering water on a high heat for about 4 minutes until it forms a thick creamy mousse. Continue beating as the mixture thickens. Add the crème fraîche and beat. Remove from the heat when it is smooth.

Pour the sabayon over the fruits and cook in the middle of the oven for 8 minutes. Place under the grill for a further 3 minutes. Serve hot, warm or cold.

Chocolate fondue

Serves 6 to 8

PREPARATION TIME: 30 minutes
COOKING TIME: 3 minutes

CHOCOLATE FONDUE
400g/14oz rich dark chocolate
100ml/3½fl oz milk
50g/2oz caster sugar
200ml/7fl oz single
crème fraîche

FOR DIPPING
1kg/2lb 4oz seasonal fruits
(pineapple, bananas, raisins,
strawberries, kiwis, cherries,
pears, apples, oranges,
clementines, apricots...)
Juice of 1 lemon (optional)
1 pound cake, 1 packet
madeleine's, or a brioche
2 packets of fine thin rolled
biscuits, e.g. cigarettes russes
1 packet marshmallows

Prepare the fruit for the filling: peel and cut into small pieces, removing the seeds and stones. Squeeze lemon over the fruit to keep from turning brown. Cut the cake and Madeleine's or brioche into small cubes and placed in pretty dessert glasses or coupes. Ensure you place wooden sticks or skewers on the table.

Make the fondue at the last minute: break the chocolate into pieces in an attractive serving bowl. Melt in the microwave or in a bowl set over a pan of simmering water. As soon as it softens add the milk, caster sugar and cream. Stir to make a smooth sauce. Let the mixture cool a little before serving.

To eat the fondue each guest picks up pieces of fruits, cake and marshmallows, alternating them to make a 'kebab' on a wooden skewers or sticks. This is then briefly plunged into the bowl filled with chocolate. If the fondue becomes too thick, add a little more cream at the table.

Exotic spiced fruit salad ▾

Serves 6
PREPARATION TIME: 20 minutes,
plus chilling time
COOKING TIME: 5 minutes

SYRUP
12 sugar lumps
200ml/7fl oz water
Juice of 1 lime
½ vanilla pod
Small pieces of cinnamon stick
1 star anise

SALAD
1 small pineapple
1 ripe mango
1 papaya
2 kiwis
Finely grated rind and
juice of 1 lime
2 bananas

Make the syrup: put the sugar lumps, water and lemon juice in a pan. Add the half vanilla pod sliced lengthways in two and scraped, the cinnamon and the star anise. Simmer for 5 minutes then leave to cool allowing the spices to infuse.

Meanwhile, make the fruit salad: Carefully skin and dice the pineapple. Peel the mango and dice the flesh into large cubes. Cut the papaya in two lengthways; remove the seeds, and the skin from the flesh and dice. Peel and dice the kiwis. Mix all the fruit in a large bowl with the finely grate rind and juice of the lime.

Peel the bananas, cut into thick slices and add to the bowl.

Pour the syrup over the fruit, straining or leaving the spices depending on your taste. Mix well, leave to cool and then cover with cling film and refrigerate for at least 2 hours.

COOK'S TIP

You can flavour the syrup with white rum. You can also serve this exotic fruit salad in individual glasses or dessert coupes with a scoop of vanilla ice cream: it's delicious!

VARIATIONS

You can make the salad using other kinds of fruit, or just one fruit, creating a huge variety of salads. You can also add tinned fruit to a fresh fruit salad. In that case mix all or part of the syrup from the tin into the salad.

Whole oranges with port ▸

Serves 8

PREPARATION TIME: 30 minutes,
plus soaking time
COOKING TIME: 1 hour 30 minutes

8 oranges
500g/1lb 2oz caster sugar
500ml/18fl oz water
250ml/9fl oz white port
Fresh coriander leaves

The day before, wash five oranges, finely grate the rind on four of them to make zest. Cut and keep a few fine slivers of rind from the fifth for decoration.

Keeping them whole, slice the remaining skin and pith off the oranges to reveal the flesh. Pack them into a pan, side by side so they will not move.

Add the caster sugar and water. Place a small plate on top of the oranges in the pan to prevent them floating. Lightly simmer on a low heat for 1 hour. Set aside to cool for about 12 hours in the syrup.

Next day, drain off the syrup and pour into a smaller pan. Blanch the orange rind by plunging into boiling water for a few moments to soften and then add it to the syrup. Cook over a low heat until reduced by half. Remove from the heat and add the port. Stir thoroughly.

Cover the oranges with the syrup and keep in the fridge until ready to serve.

Serve the oranges in individual transparent glasses, bowls or coupes and pour the syrup around them. Place the glasses on individual saucers and decorate the saucers with coriander leaves and the fine slivers of orange. Serve immediately.

Tiered apple dessert

Serves 6 to 8

PREPARATION TIME: 30 minutes ,
plus overnight soaking
COOKING TIME: 20 minutes

250g/9oz fromage blanc
75g/3oz caster sugar
½ tbsp vanilla sugar
1 large glass fruit juice
(orange, apricot or mixed,
about 100ml/3½fl oz)
15 slices brioche loaf

APPLE COMPOTE
4 firm dessert apples
50g/2oz caster sugar
½ tbsp vanilla sugar
20g/¾oz butter

DECORATION
1 apple
Juice ½ lemon
1 glace cherry

Make the apple compote: peel and quarter the apples. Remove the pips and the core and slice. Put into a pan with the caster sugar, vanilla sugar and butter. Cover and cook for 10 minutes over a low heat. Remove the lid and stir with a wooden spoon to beak up the apples and make compote. Set aside to cool.

Put the fromage blanc into a bowl with the caster sugar and vanilla sugar. Stir thoroughly to make a smooth mixture without lumps.

Pour the fruit juice into a soup plate. One by one, quickly moisten three slices of the brioche loaf and arrange in the bottom of a 16cm/6½in charlotte tin.

In the same way, one at a time, quickly moisten the other six slices and use them to line the sides of the tin.

Fill the lined tin with half of the fromage blanc, then half of the compote, then three more slices of brioche individually moistened with fruit juice. Then add layers of the remaining fromage, the rest of the compote and finish with three slices of moistened brioche. Put a plate with a weight on top of the dessert and refrigerate for 12 hours.

To serve, turn the dessert out onto a plate and decorate with finely slices of apple dipped in lemon juice and arranged in a circle with a glace cherry in the centre.

Summer fruit brochettes (kebabs)

Serves 6
(Makes 12 brochettes)
PREPARATION TIME: 40 minutes
COOKING TIME: 10 minutes

2 unwaxed lemons
8 ripe apricots
4 nectarines
2 apples
2 pears
2 bananas
1 unwaxed orange
2 tbsp flavourless oil
250g/9oz caster sugar

Squeeze the lemon. Wash and wipe dry the apricots, nectarines, apples and pears. Peel the bananas and chop into large slices. Sprinkle with lemon juice to stop them becoming black. Cut the other fruits in half to remove the stones and pips and then cut into quarters. Leave them fairly big so they don't lose shape when cooking. Sprinkle with lemon juice.

Scrub the second lemon and the orange. Slice off thin slivers of rind and squeeze the juice.

Put all the fruits in a large bowl with the citrus zest and juice. Add the oil. Macerate until needed, stirring occasionally. Before the meal stick the fruits, alternating the various types, onto brochettes and set aside. Before cooking, cover with caster sugar.

Put the brochettes under the grill or on a barbeque for about 10 minutes, turning two or three times so that they caramelise. Serve immediately.

COOK'S TIP:

You can add your choice of flavouring to this recipe by mixing a little vanilla powder or ground cinnamon to the sugar before covering the fruit with it.

Bananas en papillotes

Serves 4
PREPARATION TIME: 15 minutes,
plus soaking time
COOKING TIME: 20 minutes

2 tbsp rum
2 tbsp sultanas
4 bananas
4 tbsp caster sugar
1 tbsp vanilla sugar
½ tsp ground cinnamon
50g/2oz butter
2 tbsp pine nuts
4 scoops rum and
raisin ice cream

Put the rum and raisins into a large bowl and leave to macerate for 1 hour. When this is done, Preheat oven to Gas 9/240°C/fan oven 220°C.

Peel the bananas. Scatter the caster sugar, vanilla sugar and cinnamon onto a flat plate and roll the bananas in the mixture. Roughly chop the raisins and the butter, softened to room temperature, in an electric blender.

Cut four rectangles of aluminium foil and fold in half to double it. Put a banana onto each piece of foil. Dot with the raisins and butter. Add the remaining spiced sugar from the plate and top with pine nuts. Close and seal to form packets without squeezing the fruit. Place in the middle of the oven for about 20 minutes. Serve the bananas in their packets accompanied by scoops of rum and raisin ice cream.

Rhubarb charlotte ▾

Serves 4 to 6
PREPARATION TIME: 45 minutes,
plus overnight chilling
COOKING TIME: 20 minutes

800g/1lb 12oz rhubarb
250g/9oz caster sugar
3 gelatine leaves (6g/¼oz)
200ml/7fl oz crème fraîche
½ tbsp vanilla sugar
30 sponge fingers

COULIS
250g/9oz raspberries
100g/4oz caster sugar
Icing sugar to dust

Peel the rhubarb and chop into small pieces. Put in a pan with the caster sugar and cook for 20 minutes on a low heat, stirring from time to time to make a compote. Remove from the heat.

Meanwhile, soften the gelatine leaves by soaking in a small bowl of cold water. Wring them dry and mix with the rhubarb compote. Set aside until cold for 1 hour 30 to 2 hours.

Pour the cream into a bowl and add the vanilla sugar. Whip **(see p. 95)** then fold delicately into the rhubarb compote. Slice off the edges of the sponge fingers (so they fit together); keep the cut offs. Line the bottom and sides of a 12 to 14cm/4¾ to 5¾in charlotte tin with the biscuits, rounded side outwards. Plug any gaps with the cut offs. Fill with the rhubarb mixture. Cover with the remaining biscuits forming a star over the top. Cover the tin and place a heavy weight on top. Put in the fridge for 24 hours.

Before serving, make the coulis: carefully roll the raspberries in a damp cloth to clean. Set a few aside for decoration. Mix the raspberries and caster sugar together in a bowl. Turn the charlotte out onto a round plate and decorate with the reserved raspberries. Serve chilled accompanied by the coulis in a sauceboat. Dust with icing sugar.

Red fruit crumble ▸

Serves 6
PREPARATION TIME: 30 minutes
COOKING TIME: 30 minutes

CRUMBLE
125g/4½oz butter
125g/4½oz demerara sugar
200g/7oz flour

FILLING
500g/1lb 2oz mixed red fruit:
redcurrants, blackcurrants,
raspberries, cherries ...
100g/4oz Demerara sugar

Preheat oven to Gas 7/220°C/200°C.

Make the crumble: cut the butter into small pieces and blend with the sugar and flour, rubbing between the fingers to form fine crumbs.

Make the filling: Wash the fruit, taking them off bunches and removing stems and stones. Put them into a bowl, pour the sugar over and shake the bowl to coat the fruit.

Place the fruit in an ovenproof terra cotta, glass or porcelain 22cm/8½in bowl (like a soufflé dish), and spread the crumble mixture over the top. Place in the oven for about 30 minutes: it is ready when the crumble turns golden brown. Serve warm in its dish.

Wok fried bananas with caramel sauce

Serves 4
PREPARATION TIME: 10 minutes
COOKING TIME: 10 minutes

4 large slightly green bananas
(or 6 small ones)
1 tbsp oil
50g/2oz butter
1 tbsp flaked almonds
100g/4oz brown sugar
(soft brown or Demerara)
50ml/2fl oz golden rum
4 or 5 tbsp single cream
4 scoops vanilla ice cream

Peel the bananas, removing the strings and cut into four or five slices.

Heat the oil and butter in the wok (the oil prevents the butter burning), and fry the bananas until soft on every side.

Meanwhile, toast the flaked almonds for a few minutes in a dry non-stick frying pan. Remove the bananas from the wok and arrange on a warm serving dish. Add the brown sugar to the wok, stir with a wooden spoon and leave to caramelise. When the sauce becomes a golden syrup, pour in the rum and bring to the boil once or twice, stirring to mix.

Add the cream over a medium heat, stirring with the wooden spoon, and pour immediately over the bananas. Scattered the toasted flaked almonds over the bananas and place into four dessert bowls. Serve hot, warm or cold, as preferred, accompanied by a scoop of vanilla ice cream.

Cherry cheesecake

Serves 6-8

PREPARATION TIME: 45 minutes
COOKING TIME: 10 minutes,
plus resting time and
overnight chilling

SHORTCRUST PASTRY

100g/4oz butter
200g/7oz flour
50g/2oz caster sugar
pinch salt
Grated zest of ½ lemon
3 tbsp milk

FILLING

750g/1lb 10oz fromage blanc
175g/6oz caster sugar
1 tbsp crème fraîche
3 large eggs
1level tbsp sifted plain flour
Grates zest of 1 lemon

TOPPING

200g/7oz Morello cherries
in syrup
1 tsp potato flour

Make the shortcrust pastry: rub the butter into the flour using the tips of your fingers to make fine crumbs. Add the caster sugar, salt and lemon zest. Pile the mixture up and make a well. Pour in the milk and draw the mixture in, lightly kneading the pastry to form a ball. Put in the fridge to rest for 1 hour.

Preheat oven to Gas 6/200°C/fan oven 180°C.

Roll out the pastry line a 24cm/9in springform tin. Bake blind in the oven 10 minutes to cook the base. Remove and set aside to cool.

Reduce the oven temperature to Gas 2/150°C/fan oven 130°C. Make the filling: beat the fromage blanc, caster sugar and cream with an electric beater. Add the eggs, flour and lemon zest. Pour the mixture into the tin lined with the pastry. Cook for 1 hour, then leave to cool in the oven, without opening the door.

Remove from the oven, wait until completely cold and place in the fridge for 12 hours.

Make the topping: drain the cherries (stone as necessary) keeping the syrup. Dissolve the potato flour in half a glass of syrup, put in a pan and bring to the boil, stirring constantly. Place the cheesecake on a serving dish. Arrange the cherries on the top and cover with the thickened syrup. Serve chilled.

Roasted peaches with spiced bread

Serves 6

PREPARATION TIME: 15 minutes
COOKING TIME: 10 minutes

100g/4oz butter
6 large ripe yellow peaches
200g/7oz spiced bread, crumbled
into coarse breadcrumbs
6 tbsp peach liqueur
6 tbsp caster sugar
Peppercorns
1 lemon
6 scoops vanilla ice cream

Generously butter a baking dish with half of the butter. Preheat oven to Gas 7/220°C/fan oven 200°C.

Peel the peaches, keeping them whole. Place in the dish. Scatter the spiced breadcrumbs in the dish around the peaches. Pour a tablespoon of peach liqueur over each peach. Cover each peach with a tablespoon caster sugar, and give the peppermill couple of turns over the top.

Squeeze the lemon and sprinkle over the spiced breadcrumbs, then dot with the remaining butter. Bake for 10 minutes. Serve hot, straight from the oven. Serve a scoop of vanilla ice cream with each portion.

Baked apples

Serves 6

PREPARATION TIME: 5 minutes
COOKING TIME: 25 to 30 minutes
at ((210 changed to))
220°C/425°F (gas 7)

6 large firm dessert apples
125g/4½oz soft brown sugar
120g/4½oz butter +
20g/¾oz for the tin
50ml/2fl oz water

Preheat oven to Gas 7/220°C/fan oven 200°C. Butter an ovenproof dish large enough to hold six apples. Wash and core the apples. Use a small pointed knife make a notch in each apple about 3cm below the stem to prevent the skin bursting during cooking and then place in the buttered dish.

Insert 20g/¾oz butter and a tablespoon of brown sugar in each apple. Shake the remaining sugar over the top of the apples and dot with the rest of the butter. Pour the water into the dish. Bake in the middle of the oven for 25-30 minutes, until the apples are soft and golden brown. Serve warm or cold.

Ricotta gateau

Serves 6 to 8
PREPARATION TIME: 15 minutes
COOKING TIME: 1 hour

2 eggs
500g/1lb 2oz ricotta cheese
100g/4oz caster sugar
Pinch salt
Zest (rind) of 1 orange
100g/4oz flour
60g/2½oz raisins
30g/1¼oz candied fruit
Icing sugar to decorate

Preheat oven to Gas 6/200°C/fan oven 180°C.

Break the eggs and separate the whites and yolks. Beat the ricotta with the caster sugar and yolks. Add the salt, the finely grated orange rind and the flour. Stir in the raisins and candied fruit. Beat the egg whites until stiff and gently fold into the mixture. Pour into a deep 20cm/8in sandwich tin and cook in the oven for 1 hour.

When it is ready, remove from the oven and turn out of the tin at once. Set aside to cool. Sieve icing sugar over the gateau to decorate and serve.

Panellets

Serves 7 to 8
(Makes about 30 panellets)
PREPARATION TIME: 40 minutes
COOKING TIME: 20 minutes

1 whole egg + 2 whites
375g/13oz caster sugar
375g/13oz ground almonds
½ tsp vanilla essence
1 tbsp water
250g/9oz pine nuts
Butter for the baking sheet

Lightly beat three egg whites until barely frothy. Add the caster sugar, ground almonds and vanilla: the marzipan paste should be about the same consistency as modelling clay. Preheat oven to Gas 7/220°C/fan oven 200°C.

Use the almond paste to form small balls by hand about the size of quails' eggs. Mix the egg yolk and water together and coat the pine nuts so that they will stick to the marzipan balls. Roll the balls in the pine nuts.

Arrange the panellets on a buttered baking sheet and bake for about 20 minutes, until the pine nuts turn golden brown. Serve fairly quickly, while the balls are still soft.

Pears in red wine ›

Serves 6
PREPARATION TIME: 20 minutes
COOKING TIME: 15-20 minutes
(depending on the variety of pear)

500ml/18fl oz red wine
1 orange
75g/3oz brown sugar
2 cloves
½ vanilla pod
1 cinnamon stick
6 medium-sized firm pears

Pour the wine and the orange juice into a pan large enough to contain the pears standing upright. Add the sugar and spices and bring to the boil.

Carefully peel the pears keeping them whole and on the stems. Turn them over cut a cross right up to the centre with the point of a knife so they will open out and form a flower shape when cooked. Place in the hot spiced wine. Cover and simmer until the pears are tender. When they are ready the tip of a knife easily penetrates the flesh.

Drain the pears and place in a serving bowl. Boil the juice until there is only a large glass of it left. Pour over the pears. Serve cold.

Candied fruit diplomate

Serves 8
PREPARATION TIME: 30 minutes
plus overnight chilling
COOKING TIME: 45 minutes

30g/1¼oz butter for the tin
200g/7oz caster sugar + 1 tbsp
200g/7oz mixed candied fruit
3 tbsp kirsch
1 large brioche loaf (400g/14oz)
700ml/1¼pints milk
5 eggs
½ tbsp vanilla sugar
Candied fruits to decorate

Preheat oven to Gas 6/200°C/fan oven 180°C. Butter a 16cm/6¼in diameter charlotte tin and coat with a tablespoon of caster sugar. Put the candied fruits in a bowl with the kirsch.

Cut the brioche into 1cm/½in slices. Pour the milk into a pan and heat until simmering. Beat the eggs, caster sugar and vanilla sugar together in a bowl until it starts to become frothy. Continue beating and gradually add the hot milk. Set aside until required.

Line the bottom of the tin with slices of brioche and scatter a few of the candied fruit and a little of the kirsch over. Fill the tin, alternating layers of brioche with the candied fruit. Finish with a layer of brioche. Slowly strain the cream over and leave to soak in for a few minutes.

Place in a shallow dish half filled with boiling water and bake for 45 minutes in this bain-marie. Remove from the oven and leave to cool completely. Chill for 12 hours or overnight. To serve, turn out of the tin and decorate with candied fruit.

Lemon roulade

Serves 6
PREPARATION TIME: 45 minutes
plus chilling time
COOKING TIME: 10 minutes

LEMON CURD
1 egg + 3 yolks
125g/4½oz caster sugar
100g/4oz butter
100ml/3½fl oz limoncello
1 tbsp grated lemon rind

SPONGE ROLL
4 eggs
125g/4½oz caster sugar
60g/2½oz plain flour
40g/2¾oz cornflour
10g crystallised sugar

Make the lemon curd in advance so that it is thick enough when you need to use it and roll the sponge: Put the whole egg, yolks, caster sugar, butter and lemon juice together in a pan. Whisk the mixture until it thickens (do not let it boil). When the cream is about the same consistency as honey, pour into a bowl. Add the finely grated lemon rind. Set aside to cool and place in the fridge for 2 - 3 hours.

Make the sponge roll: Preheat oven to Gas 7/220°C/200°C. Line the baking tray with baking paper. Separate the egg yolks and whites. Beat the whites until stiff. Beat the yolks and caster sugar together until thick and creamy. Stir in the sieved flour and cornflour with a flexible spatula and delicately fold in the egg whites. Spread the mixture over the baking paper to within 2–3cm/¾–1½in of the edge and smooth the surface. Bake for 10 minutes. When cooked, the flat sponge is golden and comes away from the edge of the paper. Remove from the oven, cover with crystallised sugar turn onto a clean, damp cloth.

Remove the paper. Spread a thick layer of lemon cream over the sponge. Roll it over and over on itself taking care not to break it (the damp cloth helps to keep it flexible). Let the roll cool and then replace in the fridge for 3 to 4 hours. Cut into 1cm/½in slices to serve.

Apple gateau ▾

Serves 8 to 10
PREPARATION TIME: 1 hour
15 minutes
COOKING TIME: 1 hour 10 minutes

CAKE MIXTURE
250g/9oz butter
250g/9oz plain flour
50g/2oz caster sugar
Grated zest of 1 lemon
3 egg yolks + 1 white

FILLING
1kg/2lb 4oz firm dessert apples
4 tbsp dried breadcrumbs or
breadcrumbs from stale bread
30g/1¼oz butter

GLAZE AND DECORATION
75g/3oz currants
6 tbsp rum
2 whole eggs + 1 yolk
75g/3oz caster sugar + 2 tbsp
300ml/10fl oz crème fraîche
25g/1oz melted butter

The day before, soak the raisins in the rum. Next day make the pastry: rub the butter into the flour using the tips of your fingers. Add the caster sugar, lemon zest, egg yolks and finally the white. Bring it all together to form a soft ball of pastry. Roll out and line the bottom and sides of a deep 26cm/10¼in diameter tin. Chill until ready to use.

Preheat oven to Gas 7/220°C/fan oven 200°C.

Make the filling: peel and slice the apples. Bring the tin out of the fridge. Spread an even layer of breadcrumbs on top of the pastry, dot with butter and arrange the apples on top. Bake for 10 minutes.

Meanwhile, make the custard glaze: strain the raisins, retaining the rum. Beat the whole eggs, yolk and caster sugar. Add the crème fraîche and the rum.

When the pastry has cooked for 10 minutes spread half of this mixture over the apples and lower the oven temperature to Gas 4/180°C/fan oven 160°C and cook for 25 minutes.

Remove from the oven at once and pour the remaining mixture and the raisins over the gateau. Then sprinkle with caster sugar and pour melted butter over the top. Return to the oven and cook for a further 40 minutes: the cream should be set and the pastry cooked. Set aside until completely cold before turning out and serving.

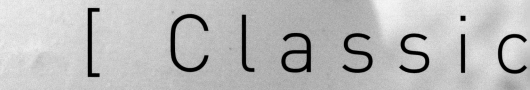

[Classic

desserts]

Our love of sweet things goes back many thousands of years. The first cake was probably made in Neolithic times: one day, someone left a mess of stewed cereal on a stone and it cooked under the sun's rays, making... a round flat biscuit! Ever since those days, desserts have continued to get better and better and have been continuously reinvented. Most great pastries and cakes were created in celebration of a special event, or in homage to a famous person, but some were discovered because of a mistake or by a lucky accident.

If the fame of certain desserts never goes beyond a specific town or a region, there are others that have achieved great acclaim around the world: these are the great classic recipes that form part of our culinary history. It is impossible to imagine a Christmas without a Yule log, Easter without a Simnel cake, nor Shrove Tuesday without pancakes. You don't need to live in Paris or Brest to savour the delights of Paris-Brest, nor in Alsace to enjoy a gugelhupf, in Germany to appreciate Black Forest Gateau or travel to Italy to indulge in a tiramisu...

Desserts have a marvellous existence, opening a world of sweet delights!

Old-fashioned crème brûlée

Serves 6

PREPARATION TIME: 15 minutes,
plus chilling time
COOKING TIME: 30 minutes

1 vanilla pod
250ml/9fl oz milk
250ml/9fl oz single or
whipping cream
4 egg yolks
30 to 50g/1¼ to 2oz caster sugar
1 tsp orange-flower water
60g/2½oz demerara sugar

Split the vanilla pod open lengthways, put in a small pan with the milk and bring to the boil. Remove from the heat at the first bubble, cover and leave to infuse for 10 minutes. Add the cream and heat until it starts to simmer. Preheat oven to Gas ½/120°C/fan oven 100°C.

Cream the egg yolks and caster sugar until they start to whiten then gradually pour the vanilla flavoured milk into the mixture. Add the orange flower water.

Divide this cream between six small ovenproof bowls. Cook in the middle of the oven for 25 minutes until a skin begins to form on the surface (don't let the cream take on any colour). Cool and chill for at least 2 hours.

To "burn" the cream, heat the grill. Place the rack about 15cm/6in below the grill. Cover the cream in Demerara sugar. Place under the grill and watch carefully as the sugar caramelises. As soon as the Demerara forms a golden crust, remove the dishes and serve immediately. If you prefer to eat them cold, let them cool before putting them in the fridge.

COOK'S TIP

You can use a specialist gas burner to caramelise the creams, in place of the grill.

Semolina and apricot gateau

Serves 6

PREPARATION TIME: 30 minutes
COOKING TIME: 30 minutes

SEMOLINA GATEAU
700ml/1¼ pints milk
1 pinch of salt
½ vanilla pod
100g/4oz finely ground semolina
75g/3oz caster sugar
50g/2oz butter + some for the tin
3 eggs

APRICOT COMPOTE
50g/2oz apricots
50ml/2fl oz water
125g/4½oz caster sugar

DECORATION
fresh apricot slices
Vanilla pod pieces

Make the semolina gateau: Bring the milk to the boil with the salt and the half vanilla pod, slit in two lengthways. Scatter the semolina onto the milk at the first sign of bubbles. Stir continuously until the semolina thickens - this will take about 3 minutes. Remove from the heat add the caster sugar and leave to cool. Add the butter and the lightly beaten eggs.

Make the apricot compote: Wash and stone the fruit. Cook in a pan with half a glass of water Add the caster sugar to the cooked fruit and mix well.

Preheat oven to Gas 6/200°C/fan oven 180°C. Butter a 24cm/9in soufflé dish and line with baking paper. Fill with half the semolina and cover with the apricot compote. Fill the rest of the dish with the remaining semolina and bake for 20 minutes. When it is cooked, remove the gateau from the oven and wait until it is cold before turning out. Remove the paper. Decorate with slices of apricot and small pieces of vanilla pod.

Chocolate mousse

Serves 6
PREPARATION TIME: 20 minutes
(make 3 hours before serving)
plus chilling time

200g/7oz rich dark chocolate
125g/4½oz butter
5 medium eggs
Pinch salt
2 tbsp caster sugar

DECORATION (OPTIONAL)
Chocolate vermicelli, chips or
grated chocolate, multicoloured
pastilles, chocolate-coated
coffee beans, whipped cream or
icing sugar

Break the chocolate into small squares. Melt in a bowl set over a pan of simmering water. Remove from the heat. Cut the butter into small pieces and add, stirring to make a smooth shiny cream.

Separate the egg white and yolks. Beat the yolks into the chocolate. Leave the resulting mixture to cool.

Beat the egg whites and salt. When they are firm and stiff, shake the sugar over and beat for a few moments to mix in thoroughly. Add a third of the whites to the cold chocolate. Beat with a wooden spoon to lighten the mixture. Place the remaining whites carefully on top, coat with the mixture and fold in delicately.

Turn the mixture into a large decorative bowl or divide between six ramekins. Chill for 2 - 3 hours. You will need to wait for about 1 hour for the mousse to set sufficiently (do not keep it for longer than 12 hours).

Before serving you can decorate the mousse with the vermicelli, chocolate chips or grated chocolate, multicoloured pastilles, chocolate-coated coffee beans, or a touch of whipped cream or icing sugar.

Meringues

Serves 6
PREPARATION TIME: 5 minutes
COOKING TIME: 1 hour 30 minutes

3 egg whites
250g/9oz caster sugar
Oil and flour for the baking paper

Cut a piece of baking paper the same size as your baking tray. Cover evenly with oil and dust with flour.

Beat the egg whites stiffly until they form firm peaks. Lightly scatter the caster sugar evenly over the whites and whisk until well combined. Scatter over more sugar and whisk until all the sugar has been incorporated.

Preheat oven to Gas ¼/110°C/fan oven 90°C. Pipe the mixture onto the papered baking tray, taking care to leave plenty of space between the individual meringues as they increase in size during cooking. Place in the middle of the oven for at least 1 hour 30 minutes. Keep an eye on the colour of the meringues: they should remain white. When they are cooked, take them out of the oven and remove the baking paper. You can eat them as they are or use them to accompany many different desserts.

Caramelised rice gateau

Serves 6
PREPARATION TIME: 20 minutes, plus resting rime
COOKING TIME: 45 minutes

250g/9oz short grain or pudding rice
1 litre/1¾ pints milk
Zest or rind of 1 unwaxed lemon
1 vanilla pod
100g/4oz caster sugar
50g/2oz butter
30 sugar lumps
4 or 5 tbsp water
4 egg yolks
100g/4oz diced candied fruit

Preheat oven to Gas 7/220°C/fan oven 200°C.

Wash the rice, put in a pan and cover with cold water. Bring to the boil and drain. Put the milk, lemon zest, vanilla pod split in two lengthways, and caster sugar into a large pan that can go in the oven and bring to the boil. Remove from the heat, add the butter and rice and return to the heat. As soon as it begins to simmer, cover with a lid and place in the oven to cook for 25 minutes.

Moisten the sugar lumps and place in a 14cm/5½in diameter charlotte tin. Place on a medium heat watching closely: when the caramel become golden, remove from the heat and taking care not to burn yourself, tip the tin ensure it is evenly coated with caramel.

Remove the vanilla pod and lemon peel from the rice and set aside to cool. Add the egg yolks and candied fruit, stir and pour into the tin.

Place the tin into another ovenproof container half-filled with hot water and cook in this bain-marie in the oven for 20 minutes. Cool and then refrigerate for 4 hours.

To serve, soak the bottom of the tin in hot water and turn out onto a serving dish.

Cherry and rhubarb clafoutis

Serves 6
PREPARATION TIME: 30 minutes
COOKING TIME: 25 to 30 minutes

300g/10oz rhubarb
300g/10oz cherries
30g/1¼oz butter
100g/4oz flour
100g/4oz caster sugar
Pinch salt
3 medium eggs
200ml/7fl oz milk
1 tbsp vanilla sugar
500ml/18fl oz vanilla ice cream

Peel the rhubarb and cut into small pieces. Wash, tail and stone the cherries. Generously butter six small individual clafoutis tins and divide the fruit between them.

Preheat oven to Gas 7/220°C/fan oven 200°C. Make the clafoutis mixture: Heat the flour in a bowl, making a well in the centre. Put the caster sugar and salt in the well and add the eggs. Begin mixing, gradually blending in the warm milk.

Put the mixture into the tins on top of the fruit and cook in the oven for 25 -30 minutes. Take out of the oven and dust with vanilla sugar. The clafoutis will collapse slightly as they cool. Serve warm or cold with a scoop of vanilla ice cream on top.

Individual egg custards ▾

Serves 6
(makes 6 x125ml/4fl oz ramekins)
PREPARATION TIME: 15 minutes
COOKING TIME: 40 minutes at
200°c/400°f (gas 6)

500ml/18fl oz milk
75g3oz caster sugar
½ vanilla pod
3 large eggs

Bring the milk, caster sugar and sliced half vanilla pod to the boil. Remove from the heat and infuse for 5 minutes then remove the vanilla.

Beat the eggs in a bowl. Continue beating and gradually add the hot milk. Strain through a fine sieve and divide between six ramekins.

Preheat oven to Gas 6/200°C/fan oven 180°C.

Cover a baking tray (or a dish large enough to hold the ramekins) with two or three layers of kitchen paper and place the ramekins on top. Fill the dish with hot water to the same level as the custard in the ramekins and place in the oven for 40 minutes. Be sure to put the dish in the upper third of the oven so that the bottoms of the ramekins do not get too hot, while the tops on the other hand, change colour. The custards are ready when they are no longer liquid. Remove from the oven and set aside to cool before serving.

Black Forest Gateau

Serves 8 to 10
PREPARATION TIME: 45 minutes
COOKING TIME: 15 minutes

GATEAU
6 medium eggs
200g/7oz caster sugar
Pinch salt
1tsp vanilla essence
60g/2½oz flour +
2 tbsp for the tin
75g/3oz cocoa powder
250g/9oz butter +
30g/1¼oz for the tin

FILLING
500g/1lb 2oz sharp cherries,
fresh or frozen
250ml/9fl oz water
175g/6oz caster sugar
2 liqueur glasses kirsch
(about 200ml/7floz)

CREAM
400ml/14fl oz crème fraîche
1 shaved ice cube (optional)
50g/2oz icing sugar
1 or 2 liqueur glasses kirsch
(about100-200ml/3½-7fl oz)

DECORATION
200g/7oz rich dark chocolate

Make the sponges: butter and flour three 18cm/7in sandwich tins. Whisk the eggs, caster sugar, salt and vanilla essence with a beater: The mixture should triple in volume to form a light mousse.

Preheat oven to Gas 5/190°C/fan oven 170°C. Mix the flour and cocoa powder together and sieve. Add this to the mixture, a couple of spoonfuls at a time. Gently melt the butter. Set aside to cool and then delicately add to the mixture. Divide between the tins and cook in the oven for 15 minutes. After checking the middle of the cakes to ensure they are cooked, remove from the oven and wait 5 minutes before turning out to cool on a wire rack.

Make the filling: if you are using fresh cherries, remove the stems and stone them. Bring the water and caster sugar to the boil. Put the cherries in simmer for 5 minutes. Drain the fruit. Let the syrup cool before adding the kirsch.

Make the cream: put the crème fraîche in a chilled bowl (if the cream is too thick, use some shaved ice to thin it). Add the icing sugar. Beat until it thickens like whipped cream. Dribble the kirsch into the mixture while continuing to beat. Chill.

Make the decoration: the chocolate should be at room temperature. Using a vegetable peeler, shave the chocolate over aluminium foil, touching it as little as possible (wear fine plastic gloves if possible). Keep the shavings in the fridge until you are ready to use them.

Construct the gateau: prick the cold sponges all over with a fork and moisten with the kirsch. Place one of them in the middle of a serving dish for the base. Spread a layer of cream 1cm/½in thick over it (about a quarter of the mixture) and spread half of the poached cherries on top. Place the second sponge on top of the cherries and repeat the procedure. Carefully put the third cake on top of the second layer of cherries. Cover the top and sides with the remaining cream. Gently scatter the chocolate shavings on the gateau, lightly pressing them into the cream before serving.

VARIATION:

You can use 500 to 600g/1lb 2oz - 1lb 5oz of tinned cherries in place of the fresh ones. Drain, and stone them before adding to the syrup with two liqueur glasses of kirsch.

Tiramisu ›

Serves 8
PREPARATION TIME: 10 minutes,
plus overnight chilling

200ml/7fl oz strong coffee
2 tbsp Marsala wine
18 sponge fingers
6 egg yolks + 3 whites
250g/9oz caster sugar
500g/1lb 2oz mascarpone cheese
2 tbsp cocoa

Mix the coffee with a tablespoon of Marsala wine. Quickly moisten the biscuits with the mixture and place in bottom of a 15x20cm/6x8in rectangular dish to form a layer.

Whip the egg whites until stiff. Cream the caster sugar and egg yolks until they begin to whiten. Add the mascarpone and remaining Marsala, mix together then delicately fold in the beaten egg whites.

Pour the cream over the biscuits and place in the fridge for 24 hours. Before serving, dust the surface of the tiramisu with the cocoa powder.

Easter Gateau with fruit and nuts

Serves 6
PREPARATION TIME: 45 minutes
COOKING TIME: 20 minutes

GENOESE SPONGE
3 medium eggs
100g/4oz caster sugar
Pinch fine salt
100g/4oz plain flour
40g/1½oz butter +
20g/¾oz for the tin

SYRUP
125ml/4fl oz water
250g/9oz caster sugar
3 tbsp brandy
100g/4oz stoned dates
50g/2oz walnut halves

ICING
100g/3½oz icing sugar
1 tbsp water
1 tbsp brandy

DECORATION
10 shelled pecan nuts
3 pistachios

Make the Genoese sponge the day before: Break the eggs into a mixing bowl and add the caster sugar and salt. Put the bowl over a pan of simmering water over a low heat. Beat with an electric whisk for 8-10 minutes until the mixture triples in volume, becoming pale yellow, smooth and creamy. Seive the flour over the surface of the mixture. Delicately mix with a wooden spoon. As soon as some of the flour is folded in, gently add the butter then quickly and lightly finish folding the ingredients in until just combined - the mixture should retain its volume.

Preheat oven to Gas 5/180°C/fan oven160°C. Put the mixture into a deep 20cm/8in sandwich tin and place in the oven for 20 minutes. Check that the cake is cooked by inserting a metal skewer into the centre of the cake: it should come out dry. When it is cooked, turn the sponge out onto a wire rack and leave to cool. Keep for 24 hours, so the cake is a little dry. Slice horizontally into three circles.

Make the syrup: pour the water and caster sugar into a pan. Boil on a low heat for 10 minutes then remove from the heat and add the brandy.

Finely chop the dates and walnuts add to the hot syrup and leave to cool. Reconstitute the cake on plate moistening each layer in the fruit syrup.

Make a thick icing with the brandy, water and icing sugar. Beat well and then use a spatula to spread over the top of the cake. Decorate with the pecan nuts halves and the chopped pistachios. Arrange red advent candles in the middle of the gateau and light before serving.

Crème caramel in ramekins

Serves 8
PREPARATION TIME: 5 minutes
COOKING TIME: 15 minutes
in the microwave

400ml/14fl oz milk
1 tsp vanilla powder
4 medium eggs
100g/4oz caster sugar
12 sugar lumps

Pour the milk into a tall microwaveable container, add the vanilla, and cook for 2 mins at maximum power. Mix the eggs and sugar lightly in mixing bowl without frothing and gradually stir in the hot milk.

Put a sugar lump and a half into each of eight ramekins 8cm/3¾in diameter and 4cm/1¾ tall. Moisten with a few drops of water and place in the microwave for about 8 minutes on full power, watch closely and stop cooking as soon as the caramel becomes golden.

Pour the custard into the ramekins and place them in a circle in a deep, round flat-bottomed porcelain dish filled two thirds full of boiling water. Cover the whole with cling film pierced a few times with a knife and cook for 5 minutes at 70 % power. Leave to rest for 5 minutes before removing from the bain-marie.

Serve the crème caramel warm or cold.

Breton Far

Serves 8 to 10
PREPARATION TIME: 20 minutes,
plus overnight soaking
COOKING TIME: 1 hour

250g/9oz soft prunes
1litre/1¾pints light tea
50g/2oz half salted butter
200g/7oz sieved flour
250g/9oz caster sugar
Pinch salt
4 medium eggs
700ml/1¼ pints warm milk
1 tbsp rum
½ tbsp vanilla sugar
1 tsp ground cinnamon

Place the prunes in a bowl and pour over the tea and leave to macerate overnight. Next day, drain and stone them.

Generously butter a 28cm/11in ovenproof terracotta or porcelain dish. Spread the prunes over the bottom.

Preheat oven to Gas 7/220°C/fan oven 200°C.

Put the flour into a mixing bowl and make a well in the centre. Add the caster sugar, salt and eggs into it and gradually stir in the milk: the mixture should be light and smooth. Add the rum and vanilla sugar.

Gently pour the mixture over the prunes. Sprinkle the cinnamon over the surface and dot with small pieces of butter.

Place in the oven for 1 hour: the far rises hugely during cooking and then falls back down. When the cooking is finished, remove from the oven and cool before serving.

Simnel cake

Serves 15
PREPARATION TIME: 30 minutes
COOKING TIME: 1 hour

225g/8oz butter +
some for the tin
225g/8oz soft brown sugar
4 large eggs
350g/12oz currants
175g/6oz raisins
330g/10½oz flour
Pinch salt
Grated rind of 1 lemon
1 tsp ground cinnamon
1 tsp grated nutmeg
250ml/9fl oz milk
500g/1lb 2oz marzipan
6 tbsp apricot jam or other fruit
jelly

The day before butter a round 20cm/8in tin with 7 to 8cm high sides and line with baking paper.

Beat the butter and soft brown sugar thoroughly until they become creamy. Add the eggs one at a time, beating them in between each addition.

Wash and drain the raisins. Preheat oven to Gas 4/180°C/fan oven160°C.

Mix the flour with the salt, lemon zest, spices and raisins and add this to the egg mixture. Add enough milk to soften the mixture without being too liquid.

Spoon half of the mixture into the prepared tin, levelling the surface.

Roll out 200g/7oz marzipan. Cut out a 20cm/8in circle and place on top of the mixture in the tin. Pour the rest of the mixture over the top and smooth the surface.

Cook in the oven for 1 hour then reduce the temperature to Gas 2½/ 160°C/fan oven 140°C and cook for a further 40 minutes until the gateau is firm to the touch. Allow to cool in the tin, turn out onto a wire rack, cover and set aside until the next day.

Next day, roll out the remaining marzipan and cut out a 20cm/8in circle.

Brush apricot jam over the surface of the fruitcake and stick the marzipan on top.

Draw a criss-cross pattern over the marzipan with the tip of a knife.

Make eleven small balls with the remaining marzipan (they symbolise the disciples with the exception of Judas). Arrange then around the cake and stick them on with a little apricot jam and serve (this fruit cake keeps for several days in a metal tin).

Clafoutis of Pears Belle-Hélène

Serves 6

PREPARATION TIME: 20 minutes
COOKING TIME: 40 minutes

20g/¾oz butter
1 tbsp crystallised sugar
120–250g/4½–9oz caster sugar
(according to taste)
6 medium-sized ripe pears
Juice of 1 lemon
60g/2½oz sieved plain flour
1 tbsp vanilla sugar

4 eggs
250ml/9fl oz single crème
fraîche
250ml/9fl oz milk

CHOCOLATE COULIS

200g/7oz rich dark chocolate
200ml/7fl oz single crème
fraîche or single cream or
UHT cream
1 tbsp caster sugar

Preheat oven to Gas 6/200°C/fan oven 180°C.

Butter a deep 24cm/9½in sandwich tin and sprinkle with the crystallised sugar.

Peel the pears keeping them whole and core from the base using a small pointed knife to remove the stringy centre and pips. Sprinkle immediately with the lemon juice to prevent them browning. Place upright in the tin, leaving space between them.

Mix the flour, caster sugar and vanilla sugar in an electric food mixer, add the eggs and beat, then the crème fraîche and finally the milk. Beat to form a runny mixture. Pour gently into the tin filling the spaces around the pears. Place in the middle of the oven for 40 minutes.

Make the chocolate sauce at the last minute: break the chocolate into squares and gently melt over a bain-marie (or in a microwave). As soon as it is soft, beat it, adding the crème fraîche and caster sugar to make a smooth creamy sauce. Keep warm over a bain-marie set on a very low heat.

To serve, cut the clafoutis into six pieces. Place into individual dessert dishes and pour chocolate sauce over. Serve the remaining sauce in a sauceboat.

VARIATION:

To make a finer clafoutis mixture use two whole eggs and two yolks in place of four whole eggs.

Gateau-madeleine

Serves 8

PREPARATION TIME: 15 minutes
COOKING TIME: 30 minutes

125g/4½oz butter +
20g/¾oz for the tin
4 eggs
250g/9oz caster sugar
½ tbsp vanilla sugar
1 unwaxed lemon
1 tsp bitter almond essence
125g/4½oz flour +
1 tbsp for the tin
Pinch salt
Multicoloured vermicelli
to decorate

Preheat oven to Gas 6/200°C/fan oven 180°C.

Melt the butter gently in a pan. Remove from the heat and cool.

Break the eggs and place the whites and yolks in separate bowls. Add the caster sugar and vanilla sugar to the egg yolks and cream the mixture until it begins to turn pale. Continue beating and add the melted butter.

Scrub the lemon. Wipe dry then finely grate the rind, adding it to the mixture along with the almond essence.

Mix the flour and salt together. Sieve this onto the surface of the egg mixture but do not mix it in.

Beat the egg whites until stiff. Put them into the mixing bowl on top of the flour and fold in with a figure of eight movement – do not overmix.

Butter and flour a 20cm/8in rectangular loaf tin. Turn it over and tap to remove excess flour and pour in the cake mixture to fill. Bake in the middle of the oven for 30 minutes. If the top of the cake cooks too quickly, cover with foil to protect it. Turn out and allow to cool on a wire rack. Before serving, decorate with the multicoloured vermicellis. Serve warm or cold.

Rice pudding with cherry compote ▲

Serves 8
PREPARATION TIME: 50 minutes,
plus chilling time
COOKING TIME: 1 hour

RICE PUDDING
200g/7oz short grain or
pudding rice
1litre/1¾ pints water
1litre/1¾ pints whole milk
300ml/10fl oz single
crème fraîche
100g/4oz caster sugar

CHERRY COMPOTE
1kg/2lb 4oz cherries
2 unwaxed lemons
200g/7oz caster sugar

Make the rice pudding: rinse the rice in cold water. Put into a pan with the water, bring to the boil and cook for 5 minutes. Drain. Tip the drained rice into another pan and add the milk, half of the cream and the sugar. Mix together and then cook on a very low heat for 30 to 40 minutes, depending on how quickly the rice absorbs the liquid. Stir frequently during cooking to ensure the rice swells properly and to prevent it sticking to the pan. When the rice is cooked and the remaining liquid is creamy remove from the heat and empty into a mixing bowl. Stir the remaining crème fraîche into the hot rice to make it creamier. Divide between individual ramekins, leave until completely cold and put in the fridge for about 2 hours.

Make the cherry compote: wash, tail, halve and stone the cherries.
Scrub the lemons. Finely grate the rind and squeeze the juice.
Put everything in a pan with the caster sugar. Cook for about 30 minutes over a low heat, stirring occasionally until it forms a compote consistency with a syrupy juice. Empty into a mixing bowl and set aside until completely cold.
To serve, turn the ramekins out onto small plates. Arrange a ring of cherries around each rice pudding and place a few on top of each to decorate.

[Glossary of terms]

Arrange ▸ to place ingredients evenly or decoratively.

Bain-marie ▸ to cook something in one container placed into or on top of another part-filled with water maintained at an even temperature just below boiling.

Base ▸ mixture, cake or pastry that forms the bottom of a finished confection.

Beat ▸ to use a whisk or beater to rapidly blend ingredients together or to incorporate air into ingredients such as egg whites or cream.

Blanch ▸ to remove the skin from certain fruits or to tenderise them by first putting into boiling and then plunging into cold water. The term is often applied to almonds and peaches.

Blend ▸ to process or purée ingredients until fine.

Butter ▸ to cover a tin, mould, tool or oven dish with a thin layer of butter in order to prevent the contents sticking to it.

Caramelise ▸ used either to signal the change from sugar into caramel or for coating a tin, mould, fruit or custard in sugar and heating to form caramel.

Chop ▸ roughly cut an ingredient into small pieces using a knife or chopper.

Clarify ▸ term used to remove the impurities from butter, or to make a jelly or syrup clear and translucent.

Coat ▸ to completely cover a dessert in a semi-liquid mixture, or in an ingredient such as sugar.

Coulis ▸ a soft fruit purée, sieved to remove pips; served as a sauce.

Cover in jam ▸ to use a brush to spread a layer of jam (or jelly) on top of a cake or dessert to improve it, by adding flavour and protecting it from drying out

Cream (butter) ▸ to soften butter by beating to give it the consistency of thick cream.

Cream (eggs and sugar) ▸ to beat egg yolks and sugar together until they thicken and become pale and creamy.

Crumb ▸ to rub butter and flour between the tips of the fingers to make a mixture that crumbles into fine grains.

Dry out ▸ to beat a mixture over the heat with a wooden spoon to remove excess moisture.

Fill ▸ to stuff a cavity or hole. Example: choux pastry with cream.

Filter ▸ to remove matter from a liquid by putting it through a sieve or strainer.

Flambé ▸ to pour warmed alcohol onto a dish and set alight.

Flavour ▸ to add flavouring to a mixture. Example: to add vanilla, chocolate or spirits to desserts and creams.

Garnish ▸ to fill a pastry case with fruit or other ingredients.

Glaze ▸ to brush pastry or other mixture with milk, beaten eggs or egg yolks and water to give a golden glaze on cooking.

Ice ▸ to cover a dessert with a mixture of icing sugar and a liquid (for example water, fruit juice, alcohol).

Incorporate ▸ to add an ingredient to a mixture and mix in well.

Infuse ▸ to soak aromatic ingredients or spices in hot liquid so the liquid acquires their flavour.

Knead lightly ▸ to use the palm of the hand to push pastry away from you to make it stick together homogenously.

Knock up ▸ to trim the edge of a piece of puff pastry with a knife to ensure they rise evenly.

Line ▸ to apply a thin layer of pastry, butter, flour or biscuit to the sides of a tin or mould. Also used to describe placing buttered baking paper inside a tin.

Macerate ▸ to soak dried, fresh or candied fruit, in alcohol or sugar to flavour.

Marble ▸ to trace parallel lines in fondant icing using an icing or piping bag equipped with a very fine nozzle containing icing in another colour and then to draw evenly spaced lines across it using the tip of a knife. Example: mille-feuilles

Melt ▸ to cause a solid to change into a liquid state by applying heat.

Moisten ▸ to add liquid to a mixture or a recipe, or to make syrup, or alcohol penetrate a dry preparation, such as a sponge.

Paste ▸ a mixture of flour and water (or other liquid) such as is used in making puff pastry.

Pastry case ▸ an unfilled tart case.

Pipe ▸ the use of a piping bag and icing mixture or an icing bag to extrude icing.

Poach ▸ to cook or heat food (fruit, egg white...) for a few minutes in simmering hot water or milk.

Prick ▸ using a fork to make small holes in the bottom of a tart to prevent the pastry rising or shrinking when cooking.

Purée ▸ to blend a mixture to a fine matter.

Reduce ▸ to cause the water in a liquid to evaporate by boiling to concentrate the flavour or volume.

Ribbon (maker a) ▸ to cream egg yolks and sugar until they form a smooth consistency, which when dribbled from a height from a spatula, forms a ribbon.

Roll out ▸ to apply a rolling pin to flatten a piece of pastry whose thickness and shape varies depending on the recipe and the type of mould used.

Score ▸ to cut slits across pastry with the tip of a knife so that it doesn't collapse during cooking.

Sift ▸ to put an ingredient through a sieve to remove lumps (for example flour, icing sugar), or to use a sieve to sprinkle icing sugar over the top of a dessert to decorate.

Simmer ▸ to keep a liquid at an even temperature, just below boiling.

Skim ▸ to remove the scum from boiling syrup, as for example, when making jam.

Slice ▸ to cut lengthwise.

Slivers ▸ extremely fine slices.

Soak ▸ to dip a cake or ingredient completely into a liquid

Strain ▸ to filter a liquid or mixture through a sieve or strainer.

Thin ▸ to dilute a mixture by adding liquid or beaten eggs.

Thicken ▸ to add starch to a mixture until it thickens.

Trim ▸ to equalise the edges of a pastry case by slicing off with a knife applied to the top of the tin.

Turn out ▸ to take something out of its tin or mould.

Well ▸ to make a heap of flour with a hole in the middle into which ingredients are added in order to blend them gently in with the fingers without letting them run out before being mixed with the flour.

Whip ▸ to use a beater, whisk or a fork to incorporate air into an ingredient.

Work ▸ to beat, or mix a mixture with a beater or spoon.

Zest ▸ citrus flavouring made by grating the rind but not the pith of citrus fruits or by removing thin slices of rind using a sharp knife.

[Index of recipes]

Andalusian gateau ... 92

Apple and hazelnut turnovers ... 34

Apple fritters ... 44

Apple gateau (Apfelkuchen) ... 129

Apricot custard tart ... 24

Apricot tricornes ... 34

Baked Alaska ... 104

Baked apples ... 125

Bananas en papillottes ... 120

Bavarian cream ... 85

Berlin doughnuts ... 45

Black-Forest gateau ... 136

Breton Far ... 139

Calfoutis of Perars Belle-Hélène ... 140

Candied fruit bombe ... 112

Candied fruit diplomate ... 128

Caramelised rise gateau ... 134

Carrot cake ... 70

Cassata ... 112

Cherry and rhubarb clafoutis ... 134

Cherry cheesecake ... 124

Cherry profiteroles ... 52

Chestnut log ... 77

Chiquenaudes ... 42

Chocolate éclairs ... 48

Chocolate fondant tart ... 30

Chocolate fondue ... 116

Chocolate hazelnut brownies ... 73

Chocolate marquise ... 82

Chocolate mousse ... 133

Chocolate terrine
  with orange slivers ... 101

Coffee meringue gateau ... 96

Crème caramel en ramekins ... 138

Custard flan ... 25

Doughnuts ... 68

Dry waffles with brown sugar ... 60

Easter egg croquembouche ... 52

Easter torte ... 76

Ester gateau with fruit and nuts ... 138

Exotic puits d'amour ... 101

Exotic spiced fruit salad ... 117

Figs with almond cream ... 82

Flambé crêpes with citrus butter ... 56

Floating islands ... 85

Fresh fig gateau ... 90

Fromage blanc gateau ... 28

Fromage blanc
  with raspberry coulis ... 98

Fruit cake ... 64

Fruit sabayon ... 116

Gateau de ménage ... 70

Gateau St Honoré ... 51

Gateau-madeleine ... 140

Gugelhupf ... 67

Hot greengages with ice cream ... 110

Iced cherry soufflé ... 108

Iced nougat with chicory coulis ... 107

Individual egg custards ... 135

Individual orange sorbets ... 110

Italian almond gateau ... 28

Lemon crêpe gateau ... 59

Lemon rulade ... 128

Lemon soufflé ... 67

Madrid churros ... 45

Melon beignets ... 42

Meringues ... 133

Mille-feuilles ... 38

Neopolitan sponge ... 89

Old-fashioned crème brûlée ... 132

Orange fondant cake ... 68

Orange tutti-frutti cups ... 107

Orange-flower waffles ... 60

Pamplona gateau ... 72

Panellets ... 126

Paris-Brest ... 48

Pear soufflé crêpes ... 59

Pears in red wine ... 126

Pound cake ... 69

Puffed almond galette ... 36

Quick fruity ice cream log ... 109

Raspberry tart gratinée ... 30

Red fruit crumble ... 122

Redcurrant amandine gateau ... 96

Rhubarb charlotte ... 121

Rhubarb ice cream ... 104

Rhubarb tart with speculoos ... 24

Rice pudding
  with cherry compote ... 141

Ricotta gateau ... 126

Roasted peaches
  with spiced bread ... 124

Rose ice cream ... 113

Rum baba ... 64

Savoyard pear rézules ... 37

Semolina and apricot gateau ... 132

Simnel cake ... 139

Small coffee pots ... 98

Spiced apple tart ... 37

Strawberry and pistachio tart ... 93

Strawberry meringue gateau ... 88

Sugar tart ... 22

Summer fruit brochettes ... 120

Summer fruit gateau ... 78

Tarte Tatin ... 22

Tiered apple dessert ... 118

Tiramisu ... 136

Vanilla crêpes ... 56

Whole oranges with port ... 118

Wok-fried bananas
  with caramel sauce ... 122

Yogurt and raisin gateau ... 72

[Credits]

Many thanks to Colette Bon, Brigitte Brigante, Michèle Carles, Christian Proust and Laurent Terrasson for their valuable help, and to all the colleagues and contributors of CEDUS who for several decades have contributed to successive versions of this work undertaken by the Centre d'études et de documentation du sucre (National Centre for the Study of Sugar), Paris.
The photographer and the stylist would like to thank patisserie Maison Degas (+33 1 45 83 80 13) for their kind assistance, William Guénéron for his valuable advice, as well as all the shops who were happy to lend us cookware and tableware: Sentou (+33 1 42 71 00 01), La Samaritaine (+33 1 40 41 20 20), Quartz (+33 1 43 54 03 00), Gargantua (+33 6 13 72 06 16), Ikéa (+33 8 25 826 826).